Discovery™

500
QUESTIONS &
ANSWERS
about absolutely everything

PaRragon

Bath · New York · Cologne · Melbourne · Delhi
Hong Kong · Shenzhen · Singapore

This edition published by Parragon Books Ltd in 2017 and distributed by

Parragon Inc.
440 Park Avenue South, 13th Floor
New York, NY 10016
www.parragon.com

This special edition was printed for Kohl's Department Stores, Inc.
(for distribution on behalf of Kohl's Cares, LLC, its wholly owned subsidiary) by Parragon, Inc.

KOHL'S
Style Number 9781474895828
Factory Number: 131076
4/17

Printed in China

CONTENTS

THE SOLAR SYSTEM:
What is a solar system?   5

STARS AND GALAXIES:
What is a galaxy?   11

COUNTRIES OF THE WORLD:
How many countries?   17

RELIGION AND CULTURE:
What is religion?   23

HISTORY:
Why was ancient Egypt so great?   29

ELEMENTS AND SUBSTANCES:
What is an element?   35

FORCES AND ENERGY:
What is energy?   41

LIFE ON THE LAND:
What is the largest land animal?   47

CONTENTS

LIFE IN THE WATER AND AIR:
What is a marine mammal?   53

PLANTS:
How many kinds of plants are there?   59

ECOSYSTEMS:
What is an ecosystem?   65

PLANET EARTH:
How do we know about what
was here before us?   71

THE EARTH'S CHANGING FACE:
What is weathering?   77

THE HUMAN BODY:
How many muscles are in the
human body?   83

INDEX   90
ACKNOWLEDGMENTS   96

WHAT IS... A SOLAR SYSTEM?

A solar system is made up of a star and all the objects orbiting or circling it. Our solar system includes the Sun, eight planets and their moons, and other balls of rock, ice, and metal, such as comets and asteroids. The Sun makes up 99% of our solar system's mass.

Our solar system began as a cloud of gas and dust and slowly took shape over billions of years. The Sun is at the center of our solar system. In turn, our solar system orbits the center of our galaxy, the Milky Way. It takes our solar system about 225 to 250 million years to complete one orbit of the Milky Way.

HOW LONG IS...

... A YEAR?

The Earth travels around the Sun every 365.24 days, which gives us our calendar year of 365 days. To make up the extra 0.24 days, we add an extra day to our calendar at the end of February in every fourth year, known as a leap year.

... A YEAR ON MERCURY?

It takes approximately 88 Earth days for Mercury to travel around the Sun—so a year on Mercury is about a quarter of an Earth year.

... A YEAR ON NEPTUNE?

Neptune is so far from the Sun that its orbit takes about 165 Earth years. So one year on Neptune lasts for 165 Earth years.

... A MONTH?

A lunar month is 29.53 days long. It takes the Moon 27.3 days to circle the Earth, but it is 29.53 days from one full moon to the next, because the Earth is also moving. Our calendar months are artificial.

... A DAY?

A day is the time the Earth takes to turn once. Our day (the solar day) is 24 hours.

HOW BIG IS...

	Diameter in miles	Surface area (million sq mi)
...THE SUN?	864,327	2,346,396
...MERCURY?	3,032	29
...VENUS?	7,521	178
...THE EARTH?	7,927	197
...MARS?	4,222	56
...JUPITER?	88,846	23,707
...SATURN?	74,898	16,448
...URANUS?	31,763	3,120
...NEPTUNE?	30,775	2,423
...THE MOON?	2,159	15

HOW BIG IS THE SUN?

Compared to the Earth the Sun is massive, but compared to other stars it's only small to medium-sized.

HOW BIG IS JUPITER?

Very big! Even though Jupiter is largely gas, it weighs 318 times as much as the Earth.

HOW BIG IS THE EARTH?

Satellite measurements show it is 24,873 miles around the equator.

WHAT IS...

...SUNSET? The Earth turns on its axis once every 24 hours. The Sun appears to rise in the east, moving across the sky to set in the west.

...SUMMER? As the Earth orbits the Sun, the hemisphere of the planet tilted toward the Sun has its summer.

... THE SOLAR CYCLE? The Sun follows a cycle of activity called the Solar Cycle, which lasts about 11 years.

... A SOLAR ECLIPSE? A solar eclipse is when the Moon moves in between the Sun and the Earth, creating a shadow on the Earth.

...THE SUN?

The Sun is the star at the center of our solar system. It was formed from a cloud of gas and dust, and material from one or more exploding stars. Light and heat from the Sun support all life on Earth.

... A SUNSPOT? Sunspots are dark blotches seen on the Sun's surface. They are dark because they are slightly less hot than the rest of the surface.

... A TRANSIT? Mercury and Venus are closer to the Sun than Earth. Occasionally they can be seen crossing, or in transit over, the face of the Sun.

...A SOLAR FLARE? Flares are eruptions on the Sun's surface that release energy into space.

...THE SOLAR WIND? The solar wind is a stream of particles constantly blowing out from the Sun.

...THE SUN'S CROWN? The Sun's crown is its corona, its glowing white-hot atmosphere.

...MOONLIGHT?

Moonlight is the Sun's light reflected off the dust on the Moon's surface.

...WAXING?

Over the first two weeks of each month, we see more and more of the Moon's bright side until full moon. As the Moon appears to grow, we say that it is waxing. As the Moon appears to shrink, we say that it is waning.

...A NEW MOON?

At the new moon, the Moon lies between the Earth and the Sun, and we catch only a crescent-shaped glimpse of its bright side.

...THE MOON?

The Moon is a rocky ball and is the Earth's natural satellite. It is held in orbit around the Earth by gravity and has circled the Earth for at least 4 billion years. It is about a quarter of the Earth's diameter.

...A LUNAR ECLIPSE?

As the Moon goes around the Earth, sometimes it passes right into Earth's shadow, where sunlight is blocked off. This is a lunar eclipse.

THE PLANETS

HOW HOT IS MERCURY?

In the day, temperatures soar to 752°F; at night they plunge to -283°F.

IS THERE LIFE ON MARS?

Images from the mountains of Mars in 2011 showed signs of flowing water, suggesting that microorganisms may be able to survive.

HOW FAST DOES JUPITER SPIN?

Despite its huge size, Jupiter's surface moves at 28,000 miles per hour—faster than any other planet!

WHY IS VENUS CALLED THE EVENING STAR?

Venus reflects sunlight so well that it shines like a star. We can see it just before sunrise and also in the evening, just after the Sun sets.

WHY IS MARS RED?

Mars is red because the surface contains iron dust. Small amounts of oxygen in the atmosphere turn this rusty.

HOW HEAVY IS SATURN?

Made largely of hydrogen, Saturn is remarkably light, with a mass of 660 billion trillion tons. If you could find a big enough bathtub to put it in, it would float.

HOW WINDY IS NEPTUNE?

Neptune's winds roar around the planet at up to 1,300 miles per hour!

WHAT'S STRANGE ABOUT URANUS?

Unlike any of the other planets, Uranus does not spin on a slight tilt. Instead, it is tilted right over and rolls around the Sun on its side, like a giant bowling ball.

WHAT IS... A GALAXY?

A galaxy is a massive system of stars, gas, and dust, held together by gravity. There are billions of galaxies scattered throughout space. Sometimes they merge or collide with each other.

Our galaxy is called the Milky Way. This is because it can be seen stretching across the night sky in a blotchy white band. This is our edge-on view of the galaxy. Since our own galaxy was the first one that astronomers knew about, they came up with the word "galaxy," which comes from the Greek word for milky.

WHAT IS THE UNIVERSE?

Scientists define the Universe as absolutely everything that physically exists. It is believed that the Universe was created by the Big Bang.

WHAT WAS THERE BEFORE THE UNIVERSE?

No one knows. Some people think there was a vast ocean, beyond space and time, of potential universes continually bursting into life or failing.

WHAT WAS THE BIG BANG?

In the beginning, all the Universe was squeezed into a tiny, hot, dense ball. The Big Bang was when this suddenly began to swell explosively, allowing energy and matter, then atoms, gas clouds, and galaxies to form.

THE BIG BANG!

WHAT IS GRAVITY?

Gravity is the invisible force of attraction between every bit of matter in the Universe, such as between the Earth and the Sun.

WHAT IS THE UNIVERSE MADE FROM?

The stars and clouds in space are made almost 100% of hydrogen and helium. Rocky planets formed from concentrations of elements such as carbon, oxygen, silicon, nitrogen, and iron.

HOW HOT WAS THE BIG BANG?

As the Universe grew from smaller than an atom to the size of a football, it cooled from infinity to 50 billion billion billion°F.

WHAT WAS THE UNIVERSE LIKE AT THE BEGINNING?

The early Universe was very small, but contained all the matter and energy in the Universe today. It lasted only a split second.

HOW DO WE KNOW WHAT THE EARLY UNIVERSE WAS LIKE?

Machines called colliders and particle accelerators can recreate conditions in the early Universe by using magnets to accelerate particles and crash them together.

WHAT IS INFLATION?

Inflation is when dramatic expansion and cooling took place just a tiny fraction of a second after the Big Bang.

HOW DID THE FIRST GALAXIES FORM?

They formed from lumps of clouds of hydrogen and helium, as concentrations within the clumps drew together.

WHAT ARE IRREGULAR GALAXIES?

Irregular galaxies are galaxies that have no particular shape at all.

WHAT ARE SPIRAL GALAXIES?

Spiral galaxies are spinning pinwheel spirals like our Milky Way.

HOW MANY GALAXIES ARE THERE?

There are currently estimated to be about 125 billion galaxies in the Universe.

ARE GALAXIES IN GROUPS?

Yes. Most galaxies are in clusters, which can form larger groups called superclusters.

WHAT ARE ELLIPTICAL GALAXIES?

Elliptical galaxies are shaped like footballs. There is no gas and dust remaining in an elliptical galaxy, so no new stars can form.

WHAT ARE...

... STARS?
Stars are gigantic glowing balls of gas, scattered throughout space. They burn anywhere from a few million to tens of billions of years.

... RED GIANTS?
Red giants are huge cool stars, formed when surface gas on a medium-sized star near the end of its life swells up.

... RED DWARFS?
Red dwarfs are small and fairly cool stars with a mass of less than 40% of that of the Sun. The majority of stars are believed to be red dwarfs.

... WHITE DWARFS?
White dwarfs are the small dense stars formed when the outer layers of a star like the Sun are blown off during the last parts of the red giant stage.

... PULSARS?
Pulsars are stars that flash out intense radio pulses every ten seconds or less as they spin rapidly.

... CONSTELLATIONS?
Constellations are small patterns of stars in the sky, each with its own name.

... CLUSTERS?
Stars are rarely entirely alone within a galaxy. Many are concentrated in groups called clusters.

... THE PLEIADES?
They are a group of over 400 stars that formed in the same cloud of dust and gas.

... DOUBLE STARS?
Our Sun is alone in space, but many stars have one or more nearby companions. Double stars are called binaries.

WHAT IS THE SUN?

The Sun is a middle-aged star. It probably formed about 4.6 billion years ago. It will probably burn for another 5 billion years and then die in a blaze so bright that the Earth will be scorched right out of existence.

WHERE ARE STARS BORN?

Stretched throughout space are vast clouds of dust and gas called nebulae. Stars are born in the biggest of these nebulae, which are called giant molecular clouds.

HOW ARE STARS BORN?

Stars are born when clumps of gas in space are drawn together by their own gravity, and the middle of the clump is squeezed so hard that temperatures trigger a nuclear fusion reaction. The heat makes the star shine.

WHICH IS THE NEAREST STAR?

The nearest star, apart from the Sun, is Proxima Centauri. It is 25 trillion miles away.

WHICH ARE THE BIGGEST STARS?

The biggest stars are known as supergiants. Antares is 700 times as big as the Sun.

WHAT IS A SUPERNOVA?

A supernova is a gigantic explosion. It destroys a supergiant star. For a few minutes, the supernova flashes out with the brilliance of billions of Suns.

WHAT ARE STANDARD CANDLES?

When measuring the distance to middle-distance stars, astronomers compare the stars' brightness to stars that they know, or 'standard candles."

A SUPERNOVA

THE BIRTH OF A STAR

HOW DO WE KNOW THE UNIVERSE IS GETTING BIGGER?

We can tell the Universe is getting bigger because distant galaxies are speeding away from us. The galaxies themselves are not moving—the space in between them is stretching.

HOW LONG WILL THE UNIVERSE LAST?

It depends how much matter it contains. If there is more than the "critical density," it may begin to contract and end in a Big Crunch. If there is much less, it may go on expanding forever.

HOW DID LIFE BEGIN?

Lightning flashes may have created amino acids, the basic chemicals of life, from the waters and gases of the early Earth. But no one knows how these chemicals were able to make copies of themselves.

WHAT SHAPE IS THE UNIVERSE?

Scientists do not yet know. Perhaps the Universe is flat, perhaps it is a curve, or perhaps even a sphere.

WHERE IS THE EARTH?

The Earth is just over halfway out along one of the spiral arms of the Milky Way Galaxy, about 30,000 light years from the center.

WHERE IS ANDROMEDA?

The Andromeda Galaxy is the closest large galaxy to the Milky Way.

IS THERE LIFE ON OTHER PLANETS?

In such a large Universe, there are probably many planets like Earth, suitable for life. No one knows if life arose on Earth by a unique chance, or whether it is fairly likely to happen if the conditions are right.

WHAT IS LIFE MADE OF?

Life is based on compounds of the element carbon, known as organic chemicals. Carbon compounds called amino acids link up to form proteins, and proteins form the chemicals that build living cells.

WHERE DID THE MATERIALS OF LIFE COME FROM?

It used to be thought that organic chemicals all originated on Earth, but many complicated compounds have been found in molecular clouds.

HOW MANY ... COUNTRIES?

There are nearly 200 countries in the world. Some of these nations rule themselves, while some are ruled by other countries. The number of countries constantly changes as some join together to make a single nation, while others break up into smaller states.

WHAT IS...

...A CONTINENT?

The big masses of land that make up the Earth's surface are called continents. The biggest continent is Asia, home to more than 3.9 billion people.

...A COUNTRY?

A country is an area of land under the rule of a single government. Its borders have to be agreed upon by neighboring countries.

... A CAPITAL CITY?

The most important city in a country is called the capital.

...A STATE?

A country is often divided into smaller regions known as states, provinces, counties, or departments.

...AN EMPIRE?

An empire is a country that rules over many other countries and nations.

...A DEPENDENT NATION?

A dependent nation is ruled by another country. There are around 38 dependent nations, including many tiny islands in the Caribbean Sea and in the Atlantic and Pacific Oceans.

...AN INDEPENDENT NATION?

Independent nations rule themselves. Currently there are more than 190 independent countries in the world.

...A GOVERNMENT?

The members of the government run the country. They pass new laws on everything from schools to hospitals and businesses.

... A DEMOCRACY?
In a democracy, people vote for a political party to make the decisions.

... A PARLIAMENT?
A parliament is a meeting place where new laws are discussed and approved.

... A HEAD OF STATE?
The most important person in a country is the head of state. This may be a king or a queen or an elected president.

... THE LAW?
Laws are a system of rules that govern everything from how we elect our leaders to how we should behave toward each other.

... A NATIONAL ANTHEM?
National anthems are played or sung to show respect to a certain country. They are often played at important occasions.

... A CURRENCY?
A currency is a money system, such as the Japanese yen or the U.S. dollar.

WHICH IS THE WORLD'S RICHEST COUNTRY?

Some economists say that Qatar, in the Middle East, is the richest country because it exports huge amounts of oil and gas.

WHICH IS THE HIGHEST CITY?

La Rinconada, in Peru, is the highest city, standing at 16,732 feet above sea level.

WHICH IS THE BIGGEST COUNTRY IN THE WORLD?

The Russian Federation, measuring more than 6.6 million square miles. It spans so many time zones, its clocks are set at 9 different times!

WHICH COUNTRY HAS THREE CAPITALS?

South Africa. Cape Town is the legislative capital. Pretoria is the executive capital. Bloemfontein is the judicial capital.

WHICH IS THE OLDEST NATIONAL FLAG?

Denmark's is the oldest flag still in use. It is a white cross on a red background and was first used in the fourteenth century.

WHICH IS THE WORLD'S OLDEST ROYAL FAMILY?

The Japanese royal family has produced a long line of 125 reigning emperors over thousands of years.

WHICH IS THE WORLD'S OLDEST PARLIAMENT?

The oldest parliament is in Iceland. Called the Althing, it was started by Viking settlers in AD 930.

WHICH CITY IS A MEGACITY?

Tokyo is an example of a megacity, encompassing 26 other cities and 5 towns.

WHICH COUNTRY FITS INSIDE A CITY?

The world's smallest nation is an area within the city of Rome, in Italy. It is called Vatican City and is the headquarters of the Roman Catholic Church.

WHICH CITY IS NAMED AFTER A GODDESS?

Athens, the capital of Greece, shares its name with an ancient goddess named Athena. Her beautiful temple, the Parthenon, still towers over the modern city.

HOW MANY LANGUAGES ARE THERE?
Around 6,900 languages are spoken in the world.

WHAT IS THE MOST SPOKEN LANGUAGE?
Mandarin Chinese is spoken by the most people. Around a billion people use it every day.

DOES EVERYBODY IN ONE COUNTRY SPEAK THE SAME LANGUAGE?
Not often. For example, families from all over the world have made their homes in the U.S.

HOW MANY PEOPLE SPEAK ENGLISH?
English is the most widespread language: 470 million English-speakers are dotted through every single country.

COULD WE INVENT ONE LANGUAGE FOR THE WHOLE WORLD?
It's already been done! A language called Esperanto was invented over 100 years ago.

HOW DO WE TALK THROUGH SPACE?
Satellites are machines sent into space to circle the Earth. They can pick up telephone, radio, or television signals from one part of the world and beam them down to another.

DO WE ALL READ LEFT TO RIGHT?
The Arabic language is read right to left, and traditional Japanese top to bottom.

WHAT IS THE MOST UNUSUAL WAY TO COMMUNICATE?
In some parts of Central America, Turkey, and the Canary Islands, people figured out a way of communicating using whistles instead of words.

WHAT IS THE LEAST SPOKEN LANGUAGE?
Fewer than 20 people in Latvia speak a language called Liv.

CAN WE TALK WITHOUT WORDS?
People who are unable to hear or speak can use sign language to communicate.

WHAT IS BODY LANGUAGE?
Movements of the head and hands can be a kind of language. But be careful—shaking the head can mean yes in some countries and no in others!

WHAT IS ... RELIGION?

The world's main religions include Islam, Hinduism, Buddhism, and Judaism. The religion with the most believers—a third of the world's population—is Christianity. All faiths have their own beliefs about the nature of the world and special ways of praying and worshipping.

Most religions set down moral codes that say how believers should behave. These rules might govern how we should treat people and animals. Religious scriptures, or holy books, also tell believers how they should worship, through prayer, fasting, or pilgrimage.

WHAT IS...

...THE TAO? Pronounced "dow," it means "the way." It is the name given to the beliefs of the Chinese thinker Laozi, who lived about 2,500 years ago. Taoists believe in the harmony of the Universe.

...SHINTO? This is the ancient religion of Japan. At its holy shrines, people pray for happiness and to honor their ancestors.

...DIWALI? This is the time in the fall when Hindus celebrate their New Year and honor Lakshmi, goddess of good fortune. Candles are lit and people give each other cards and presents.

...HANUKKAH? Hanukkah celebrates the recapture of the temple in Jerusalem in ancient times. This Jewish festival of light lasts eight days, with families lighting a new candle each day.

...RAMADAN? Ramadan is the ninth month of the Muslim year. During Ramadan, people fast from sunrise to sunset, meaning they don't eat or drink between these times.

...LENT? Lent is the period before Easter that in the Christian Church remembers Jesus Christ's fasting in the wilderness.

...CHRISTMAS? Christmas is the annual Christian festival celebrating Jesus Christ's birth, held on December 25.

WHAT ARE THE FIVE "K"S?

Sikh men honor five religious traditions. Kesh is uncut hair, worn in a turban. They carry a Kangha or comb, a Kara or metal bangle, and a Kirpan or dagger. They wear an undergarment called a Kaccha.

WHAT ARE PARSIS?

The Parsis belong to a sect of the Zoroastrian religion, which began long ago in ancient Persia, now Iran. Today, Parsis live in India and Pakistan.

... A POW-WOW?

It means "a get-together." The Native American peoples of the United States and the First Nations of Canada meet up at pow-wows each year to celebrate their traditions with dance and music.

... CARNIVAL?

In ancient Rome, there was a rowdy winter festival called Saturnalia. People copied this idea in the Middle Ages, feasting before Lent began. People still celebrate Carnival today.

... BATIK?

Batik is a way of making pretty patterns on cloth. Wax is put on the fiber so that the dye sinks in only in certain places. Batik was invented in Southeast Asia.

...A KILT?

The kilt is a knee-length skirt based on traditional male dress in the Highlands of Scotland. Kilts are woven in tartan patterns that are linked with particular families or regions.

... MORRIS DANCING?

Morris dancing is an English folk dance that may date back to the fifteenth century. The dancers jingle bells tied to their legs in time to traditional music.

... KABUKI?

Kabuki is a type of drama that became popular in Japan in the 1600s and can still be seen today. The actors, who are always male, wear striking makeup and costumes.

... SUSHI?

Sushi is considered a great delicacy in Japan. It is rice wrapped in sheets of seaweed and topped with meat, fish, or vegetables.

WHO...

...WEARS GREEN ON ST. PATRICK'S DAY?

St. Patrick's Day, on March 17, is the national day of Ireland. It is celebrated all over the world, wherever Irish people have settled.

...EATS SPIDERS?

Spiders are a delicacy in Cambodia. The tastiest are plucked straight from their burrow and fried with dashes of garlic and salt.

...ARE THE TRUE CLOGGIES?

A hundred years ago wooden shoes, or clogs, were worn in many parts of Europe. The most famous clogs were Dutch, and they are still worn today by farmers and market traders in the Netherlands.

... GETS TO SIT IN THE LEADER'S CHAIR?

In Turkey, April 23 is Children's Day. One child gets the chance to sit at the desk of the country's prime minister!

... RIDES TO THE FERIA?

Each April, the people of Seville, in Spain, ride on horseback to a fair by the Guadalquivir River. They wear traditional finery and dance all night.

... DANCES A HAKA?

Maori people in New Zealand dance the haka, traditionally danced by warriors to bring them strength to face battle.

... REMEMBERS THE FIFTH OF NOVEMBER?

People in Great Britain. The date recalls the capture of Guy Fawkes, who plotted to blow up the Houses of Parliament in London in 1605. The night is marked by fireworks and bonfires.

...WEARS FEATHERS TO A SINGSING?

A sing-sing is a big festival in Papua New Guinea. Men paint their faces and wear ornaments of bone and shell and long bird-of-paradise feathers.

... PLAYS THE PANS?

People in the Caribbean play the "pans," or steel drums, at Carnival time.

... EATS THE MOST CHEESE?

The Greeks eat the most cheese, with the average person consuming 49 pounds every year. Three-quarters of this is feta cheese, made from ewe and goat milk.

... INVENTED NOODLES?

Some people say that the traveler Marco Polo brought the secret of noodle-making back to Italy from China in the Middle Ages. Others say the Romans were making pasta in Italy long before that.

... SINGS IN BEIJING?

Beijing opera is a spectacular performance. Musicians clash cymbals and actors sing in high voices. With painted faces and beautiful costumes, they take the parts of heroes and villains in ancient Chinese tales.

...WROTE A POEM TO HIS HAGGIS?

Robert Burns, the great Scottish poet. Haggis is a traditional Scottish dish made of lamb's heart, liver, and lungs, suet, onions, and oatmeal, all cooked inside a sheep's stomach.

... PAINTS THE DREAMTIME?

Australia's Aboriginals look back to the Dreamtime, a magical age when the world was being formed. Many paintings show the landscape and how it was molded by animals.

... MAKES PICTURES FROM SAND?

The Navajo people of the southwestern United States make beautiful patterns using many different colored sands.

WHERE...

... DO THEY DANCE LIKE THE GODS?

Kathakali is a kind of dance-drama performed in Kerala, southern India. Dancers in makeup and costumes act out ancient tales of gods and demons.

... ARE THERE 3 MILLION WORKS OF ART?

At St. Petersburg in Russia, in an art gallery made up of two great buildings, the Hermitage and the Winter Palace.

... DO DRAGONS DANCE?

At Chinese New Year, or Spring Festival, a dragon weaves along the street, held up by people crouching underneath it.

... DO SOLDIERS WEAR SKIRTS?

Guards of honor in the Greek army are called Evzónes. Their uniform is based on the old-fashioned costume of the mountain peoples—a white skirt, woolen leggings, and a cap with a tassel.

... DO PANAMA HATS COME FROM?

They were first made in Ecuador, braided from the leaves of the toquilla palm. But they were first exported, or shipped abroad, from Panama.

... IS THE CAPITAL OF FASHION?

Paris, in France, has been the center of world fashion for hundreds of years. Milan, London, New York, and other cities also stage fashion shows.

... DO DRUMS TALK?

In Senegal and Gambia, in Africa, the tama is nicknamed the "talking drum." Its tightness can be varied while it is being played, making a strange throbbing sound.

WHY WAS...

ANCIENT EGYPT SO GREAT?

Ancient Egypt was one of the greatest civilizations in history. It developed along the Nile River, in northeast Africa. Under the rule of kings known as pharaohs, the Egyptians made great leaps of progress in building, art, and science. Many of their monuments and tombs are still standing today, some 4,000 years later!

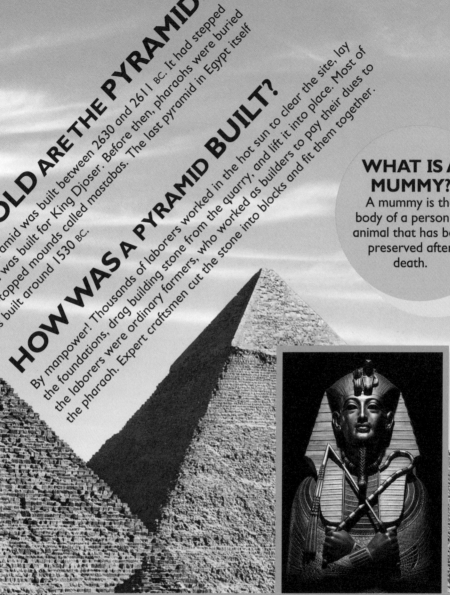

HOW OLD ARE THE PYRAMIDS?

The first pyramid was built between 2630 and 2611 BC. It had stepped sides and was built for King Djoser. Before then, pharaohs were buried in flat-topped mounds called mastabas. The last pyramid in Egypt itself was built around 1530 BC.

HOW WAS A PYRAMID BUILT?

By manpower! Thousands of laborers worked in the hot sun to clear the site, lay the foundations, drag building stone from the quarry, and lift it into place. Most of the laborers were ordinary farmers, who worked as builders to pay their dues to the pharaoh. Expert craftsmen cut the stone into blocks and fit them together.

WHAT IS A MUMMY?

A mummy is the body of a person or animal that has been preserved after death.

WHY WERE PYRAMIDS BUILT?

The pyramids are huge tombs for pharaohs and wealthy people. The Egyptians believed that dead people's spirits could live on after death if their bodies were carefully preserved. It was specially important to preserve the bodies of dead pharaohs because their spirits would help the kingdom of Egypt to survive. So they made dead bodies into mummies and buried them in these splendid tombs along with clothes and jewels.

WHY DO WE LEARN ABOUT ANCIENT GREECE?

From the eighth century BC, a great civilization began to grow in Greece, allowing architects, thinkers, and artists to thrive.

WHY DID GREEK TEMPLES HAVE SO MANY COLUMNS?

The style may have been copied from ancient Greek palaces, which had lots of wooden pillars to hold up the roof.

WHO WAS APHRODITE?

Aphrodite was the Greek goddess of love.

WHY DID THE GREEKS BUILD SO MANY TEMPLES?

Because they worshipped so many different goddesses and gods! The Greeks believed each god needed a home where its spirit could live. Every god had special powers, which visitors to the temple prayed for.

WHAT WAS SPECIAL ABOUT GREEK ARCHITECTURE?

Greek architecture was based on balance and order.

WHAT WERE THE ORIGINAL OLYMPIC GAMES?

In 776 BC, the Greeks set up an athletics competition in the city of Olympia. It was held every four years. Athletes traveled from all over Greece to compete.

DID THE ROMANS HAVE CENTRAL HEATING?

Yes. They invented a system called the hypocaust. Air heated by a wood-burning furnace was circulated through pipes underneath the floor.

WHO WAS ZEUS?

According to the ancient Greeks, Zeus was the god of the sky.

WHY DID THE ROMAN EMPEROR HADRIAN BUILD A WALL?

By the third century BC, the Romans controlled an empire from Britain to North Africa. To help guard its frontiers, Emperor Hadrian ordered a wall to be built across the north of Britain.

WHO WERE ROMAN CENTURIONS?

Centurions were army officers. They wore a decorated metal breastplate and a helmet topped with a crest of horsehair.

WHEN WERE THE MIDDLE AGES?

When historians talk about the Middle Ages, or the Medieval period, they usually mean the time from the collapse of the Roman Empire, around AD 500, to around 1500.

WHAT IS ISLAM? The religious faith taught by the Prophet Muhammad, who lived in Arabia from AD 570 to 632. People who follow the faith of Islam are called Muslims.

WHEN DID THE ISLAMIC WORLD LEAD THE GLOBE?

From about AD 700 to 1200, the Islamic World experienced a period of great power. It led the rest of the globe in learning, invention, and architecture.

WHAT WERE THE CRUSADES?
A series of wars fought between Christian and Muslim soldiers for control of the area around Jerusalem. The Crusades began in AD 1095 and ended in 1291, when Muslim soldiers forced the Christians to leave.

WHO WERE THE MONGOLS?
They were nomads who roamed over Central Asia. In AD 1206, the Mongol tribes united under a leader known as Genghis Khan and set out to conquer the world.

WHO WERE THE INCAS?
A people who lived in the Andes Mountains of South America (part of present-day Peru and Ecuador). They ruled a mighty empire from the early fifteenth century to early sixteenth century.

HOW DID THE MAYA, AZTECS, AND INCAS LOSE THEIR POWER?

They were conquered by soldiers from Spain, who arrived in America in the early sixteenth century, looking for gold.

WHY WERE LLAMAS SO IMPORTANT?

Because they could survive in the Incas' mountain homeland, where it is cold and windy, and few plants grow. The Incas wove cloth from llama wool and used llamas to carry loads up steep paths.

HOW DID SAILORS HELP SCIENCE?

European sailors often observed the plants, fishes, and animals as they traveled and brought specimens home with them. When Captain James Cook explored the Pacific Ocean, he took artists and scientists to record what they saw.

WHO WAS THE FIRST TO SAIL AROUND THE WORLD?

In 1519, a Portuguese explorer named Ferdinand Magellan sailed westward from Europe but was killed fighting in the Philippines. His captain, Juan Sebastián Elcano, managed to complete the voyage and returned home in 1522.

WHO WERE THE FIRST PEOPLE TO DISCOVER NEW ZEALAND?

The Maoris. They began a mass migration from other Pacific Islands in about 1150, but remains dating back to AD 800 have been found in New Zealand.

WHO WERE THE FIRST EUROPEANS TO SETTLE IN NORTH AMERICA?

Spanish colonists, who settled in present-day Florida and California from about 1540.

DID THE ABORIGINALS ALWAYS LIVE IN AUSTRALIA?

No, they probably arrived from Southeast Asia about 60,000 years ago.

WHO LIVED IN TENTS ON THE GREAT PLAINS?

Native American hunters, such as the Sioux and the Cheyenne. After Europeans settled in America, bringing horses with them, Native Americans spent summers on the grasslands of the Great Plains, following herds of buffalo, which they killed for meat and skins. In winter, they camped in sheltered valleys.

WHY DID THE PILGRIMS LEAVE HOME?

The Pilgrims were a group of English families with strong religious beliefs, who quarreled with Church leaders and the government. In 1620, they sailed to America to build a new community where they could practice their religion in peace.

WHAT WAS THE INDUSTRIAL REVOLUTION?

The Industrial Revolution was a huge change in the way people worked and goods were produced. Machines in large factories replaced craftspeople working by hand. It began around 1750 in Britain and spread slowly to Western Europe and the U.S.

WHY WAS STEAM POWER SO IMPORTANT?
A steam engine can do work—such as powering machines or trains—using hot steam. Steam power allowed quicker production of goods in factories and swift transportation to buyers.

WHAT WAS THE GREAT EXHIBITION?
It was a chance for Britain to show off its industrial achievements. Held in London in 1851, it was viewed by 6 million visitors from around the world.

WHAT WAS THE GREAT STINK?
It was a time during the summer of 1858 when London smelled particularly bad. Stinky sewage filled the streets and river.

WHEN DID THE FIRST TRAINS RUN?
The first passenger railroad was opened in the north of England in 1825. Its locomotives were powered by steam and replaced horse-drawn railroad wagons.

WHAT WAS STEPHENSON'S ROCKET?
In 1829, the railroad engineer George Stephenson built a groundbreaking steam locomotive called the Rocket.

WHO WORKED IN THE FIRST FACTORIES?
Thousands of poor men and women moved from the countryside to live in factory towns. They hoped to find regular work and more pay.

DID CHILDREN LEAD BETTER LIVES THEN?
No. Many worked 16 hours a day in factories or down mines. Many were killed in accidents with machinery.

HOW DID THE RAILROADS CHANGE PEOPLE'S LIVES?
They carried materials to factories and finished goods to shops. They also carried fresh foods from farms to cities and made it easier for people to travel.

WHAT IS... AN ELEMENT?

An element is a substance that cannot be split into other substances. Water is not an element because it can be split into the gases oxygen and hydrogen. Oxygen and hydrogen are elements because they cannot be split.

WHAT ARE...

... SUBSTANCES?

Substances can be solids, liquids, or gases. Substances move from one state of matter to another when they are heated or cooled, boosting or reducing the energy of their particles.

... LIQUIDS?

In liquids, particles move around a bit, so liquids can flow into any shape, while their volume stays the same.

... SOLIDS?

In solids, particles are locked together, so solids have a definite shape and volume.

... GASES?

In gases, particles zoom about all over the place, so gases spread out to fill containers of any size or shape. Gases can expand and contract depending on pressure and temperature.

WHAT HAPPENS IN EVAPORATION?

Evaporation happens when a liquid is warmed up and changes to a vapor. Particles at the liquid's surface vibrate so fast they escape altogether.

WHAT IS...

...A MOLECULE?
A molecule is the smallest part of a substance that can exist on its own.

...A PROTON?
A particle inside an atom's nucleus. It has a positive electrical charge.

...A NEUTRON?
Another kind of particle inside the nucleus. It has no electrical charge.

...AN ELECTRON?
Negatively electrically charged particles inside a nucleus.

...AN ELECTRON SHELL?
Electrons are stacked around the nucleus at different levels or "shells."

...ATOMIC NUMBER?
Every element has its own atomic number. This is the number of protons in its nucleus, balanced by the same number of electrons.

...ATOMIC MASS?
Atomic mass is the "weight" of one whole atom of a substance. It includes both protons and neutrons.

...THE PERIODIC TABLE?
Elements can be ordered into a chart called the periodic table. Columns are called groups; rows are called periods.

...THE LIGHTEST ELEMENT?
The lightest element is hydrogen. It has an atomic mass of just one.

...A NOBLE GAS?
The noble gases do not easily react with other elements.

CAN ATOMS JOIN TOGETHER?

Yes! Electrons are held to the nucleus by electrical attraction, because they have an opposite electrical charge to the protons in the nucleus. But electrons can also be drawn to the nuclei of other atoms. This is when bonding takes place.

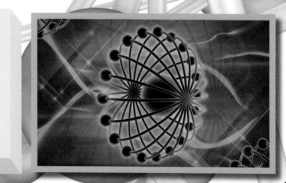

WHAT IS...

... A COMPOUND?	Compounds are substances made from two or more elements joined together.
... A MIXTURE?	Mixtures are substances that contain several chemical elements or compounds mixed together but not chemically joined.
... A METAL?	A metal is hard, dense, and shiny, and goes "ping" when you strike it with another metal. It also conducts, or transfers, electricity and heat well.
... AN ION?	An ion is an atom that has either lost one or a few electrons, or gained a few. Ions usually form when substances dissolve in a liquid.
... ELECTROLYSIS?	Electrolysis is a means of separating compounds by passing an electric current through them.
... PRESSURE?	Pressure is the amount of force pressing on something. Air pressure is the force with which air presses.
... ORGANIC CHEMISTRY?	Organic chemistry is the study of carbon and its thousands of different compounds.
... DNA?	DNA is deoxyribonucleic acid found inside every living cell. DNA provides the instructions for all the cell's activities and for the life plan of the entire organism.
...A CARBON CHAIN?	Carbon atoms often link together, like the links of a chain, to form very long, thin molecules.

HOW ...

... DO CHEMICALS REACT?

When substances react chemically, their atoms, ions, and molecules interact to form new combinations. Nearly all chemical reactions involve a change in energy, usually heat, as the bonds between particles are broken and formed.

... DOES PRESSURE CHANGE?

If you squeeze a gas into half the space, the pressure doubles (as long as the temperature stays the same). This is Boyle's Law. If you warm up a gas, the pressure rises in proportion (as long as you keep it the same volume). This is the Pressure Law.

... DO THINGS DISSOLVE?

When solids dissolve in liquid, it may look as if the solid disappears. Its atoms, ions, or molecules are, in fact, still intact—but are separated and evenly dispersed throughout the liquid.

... DO BATTERIES WORK?

Batteries create electric currents from the reaction between two chemicals, one forming a positive electrode, or conductor of electricity, and the other a negative. The reaction creates an excess of electrons on the negative electrode, producing a current.

... DOES BREAD RISE?

Bakers add yeast, a type of fungus, to dough before they put it in the oven. When it is heated, yeast reacts with the sugar in the dough to make carbon dioxide. This gas forms pockets in the bread, making it rise.

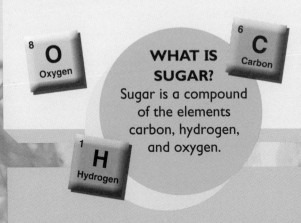

WHAT IS SUGAR?
Sugar is a compound of the elements carbon, hydrogen, and oxygen.

WHAT ARE CLOUDS?

Clouds form when warm air is heated by the Sun and rises. As it rises, the warm air cools, eventually becoming cold enough for the water vapor it contains to condense into water droplets, which we can see as clouds.

WHAT IS THE SEA MADE OF?

The sea is water with oxygen, carbon dioxide, nitrogen, and various salts dissolved in it.

WHAT IS FIRE?

Fire is a chemical reaction in which a substance gets so hot that it combines with oxygen in the air. The flames we see are the heat and light energy created by the reaction.

WHO...

... DISCOVERED RADIUM?

The Polish-French physicist Marie Curie (1867–1934) was the first woman to win not one, but two, Nobel Prizes. The first, in 1903, was for her part in the discovery of radioactivity, and the second, in 1911, for her discovery of the elements polonium and radium.

... FIRST SPLIT THE ATOM?

In 1919, the physicist Ernest Rutherford managed to break down nitrogen atoms into hydrogen and oxygen. In 1932, his students John Cockcroft and Ernest Walton managed to split the nucleus of an atom by firing protons at it.

... WAS HANS GEIGER?

Hans Geiger (1882–1945) was a German physicist who contributed toward the invention of the Geiger counter. The counter measures radioactivity by detecting alpha, beta, and gamma rays.

... DISCOVERED THE SHAPE OF DNA?

The discovery in 1953 that every molecule of DNA is shaped like a twisted rope ladder, or "double helix," was one of the great scientific breakthroughs of the twentieth century. Maurice Wilkins and Rosalind Franklin did the groundwork for the discovery. Francis Crick and James Watson, two young researchers at Cambridge University, U.K., had the inspiration and won the Nobel Prize.

WHAT IS... ENERGY?

Energy takes many forms. Heat energy boils water, keeps us warm, and drives engines. Chemical energy fuels cars. Electrical energy drives machines and keeps lights glowing. Light itself is a form of energy. Almost every form of energy can be converted into other forms. But whatever form it is in, energy is essentially the capacity for making something happen.

Nearly all our energy comes from the Sun. We get some directly by using solar power cells to trap the Sun's heat. Most comes indirectly via fossil fuels (coal and oil), which got their energy from the fossilized plants of which they are made.

WHAT IS...

... POWER?

Power is the rate at which work is done. A high-powered engine is an engine that can move a great deal of weight very quickly. Power is also the rate at which energy is transferred. A large amount of electric power might be needed to heat a large quantity of water.

... FORCE?

A force makes something move, by pushing or pulling it. Gravity is an invisible force. Other forces, such as a kick, we can see. Forces work in pairs.

... MASS?

Mass is the amount of matter in an object. It is the same wherever you measure it, even on the Moon.

...WEIGHT?

Weight is a measure of the force of gravity on an object. It varies according to where you measure it.

... SPEED?

Speed is how fast something is going.

...VELOCITY?

Velocity is how fast something is going and in which direction.

...ACCELERATION?

Acceleration is how fast something gains speed. The larger the force and the lighter the object, the greater the acceleration.

... INERTIA?

Inertia is the tendency of things to stay still unless they are forced to move.

... MOMENTUM?

Momentum is the tendency of things to keep going once they are moving, unless forced to stop or slow.

... A TURNING FORCE?

When something fixed in one place, called a fulcrum, is pushed or pulled elsewhere, it turns around the fulcrum. When you push a door shut, that push is the turning force and the hinge is the fulcrum.

... UNIFORM MOTION?

Uniform motion is when an object carries on traveling at the same speed in the same direction.

WHAT IS ... ELECTRICITY?

WHAT IS AN ELECTRIC CURRENT?

A current is a continuous stream of electrical charge. It happens only when there is a complete, unbroken "circuit" for the current to flow through.

Electricity is the presence of electric charge. This charge is carried by electrons and protons in atoms. Electrons have a negative charge and protons a positive one. Electricity can be created naturally, as in lightning, or be manmade, as with a battery.

WHAT MAKES LIGHTNING FLASH?

Lightning is created when raindrops and ice crystals inside a thundercloud become electrically charged as they are flung together. Negatively charged particles build up at the cloud's base, then discharge as lightning.

HOW DO ELECTRIC CURRENTS FLOW?

The charge in an electric current is electrons that have broken free from their atoms. None of them move very far, but the current is passed on as they bang into each other like rows of marbles.

WHAT IS A VOLT?

Electrical current flows as long as there is a difference in charge between two points in the circuit. This difference is measured in volts. The bigger the difference, the bigger the voltage.

WHAT IS RESISTANCE?

Resistance is a substance's ability to block a flow of electric current. Insulators, such as the plastic around electrical wires, are used for this reason.

WHAT ARE THE BEST CONDUCTORS?

The best conductors are metals like copper and silver. Water is also a good conductor. Superconductors are materials like aluminum.

WHAT MAKES YOUR HAIR STAND ON END?

When you comb dry hair, electrons are knocked off the atoms in the comb. Your hair is coated with these negative electrical charges and is attracted to anything positively charged.

HOW DOES A LIGHTBULB WORK?

An electric bulb has a very thin filament of tungsten wire inside a glass bulb filled with argon or nitrogen gas. When current flows through such a thin wire, the resistance is so great that the wire heats up and glows brightly.

WHAT IS A SILICON CHIP?

A silicon chip is an electronic circuit implanted in a small crystal of semiconducting silicon. This led to the manufacture of the microprocessors that make computers work.

WHAT IS HEAT?

Heat is a form of energy caused by the movement of molecules. It is created by chemical reactions, such as fire; nuclear reactions, such as in the Sun; and when other forms of energy, such as electrical or mechanical, are converted.

HOW IS TEMPERATURE MEASURED?

Temperature is usually measured with a thermometer. Some thermometers have a metal strip that bends according to how hot it is. But most contain a liquid, such as mercury, in a tube. As it gets warmer, the liquid expands and its level rises in the tube. The level of the liquid indicates the temperature.

WHAT IS TEMPERATURE?

Temperature is a measure of how fast all the molecules are moving in order to provide heat.

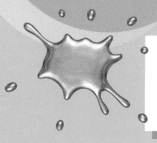

HOW DOES THE SUN GENERATE HEAT?

The Sun generates heat by nuclear fusion and radiates it in waves, which we see and feel as sunlight.

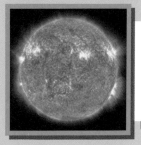

WHAT IS ABSOLUTE ZERO?

Absolute zero is the coldest possible temperature, the temperature at which atoms stop moving altogether. This happens at -459.67°F, or 0 on the Kelvin scale.

WHAT IS THE LOWEST TEMPERATURE EVER RECORDED?

Earth's lowest air temperature ever measured was -128°F. It was recorded in Antarctica. The lowest temperature ever measured was half a billionth of a degree above absolute zero.

WHAT IS LIGHT?

There are many sources of light, including the Sun, lightbulbs, and flames. When light hits an object, it can be reflected, absorbed, or bent. The study of light, known as optics, has allowed scientists to discover how we see things.

HOW IS LIGHT BENT?

Light rays are bent when they are refracted. This happens when they strike a transparent material like glass or water at an angle.

WHEN IS THE SUN RED?

When the Sun is low in the sky, sunlight reaches us after passing through the dense lower layers of the atmosphere. Particles in the air absorb shorter, bluer wavelengths of light, leaving just the red.

WHAT ARE PHOTONS?

Photons are tiny particles of light. There are billions of them in a single beam of light.

WHAT ARE THE COLORS OF THE RAINBOW?

The colors of the rainbow are all the colors contained in white light: red, orange, yellow, green, blue, indigo, violet.

WHY IS THE SKY BLUE?

Air molecules reflect more blue from sunlight toward our eyes than the other colors of visible light. This makes the sky appear blue.

WHAT'S THE FASTEST THING IN THE UNIVERSE?

Light, which travels at 186,000 miles per second!

HOW DO FIBEROPTIC CABLES WORK?

These cables don't bend light, but reflect it around corners. Inside a cable are lots of bundles of glass fibers. Light rays zigzag along the inside of each fiber, reflecting first off one side, then the other.

HOW DO YOUR EYES SEE THINGS?

The Sun and electric lights shine light rays straight into your eyes. Everything else you see by reflected light, by light rays that bounce off things. So you can see something only if there is a light source throwing light onto it.

WHAT IS...

... SOUND?

Every sound is created by vibration. Sound reaches your ears as a vibration that travels through the air.

... A SOUND WAVE?

When a sound source vibrates to and fro, it pushes the air around it to and fro in a ripple effect. This moving stretch and squeeze of air is called a sound wave.

... FREQUENCY?

Sounds differ in pitch depending on the frequency of the sound waves. If the waves follow rapidly after each other, they make a high sound. If they are far apart, they make a low sound.

...VOLUME?

The volume of a sound is the amount of pressure exerted by a sound source on air molecules. The higher the pressure, the harder the molecules will collide and the farther they will travel.

... RESONANCE?

An object tends to vibrate freely at the same rate. This is its natural frequency. If you can keep the object vibrating at the same rate as its natural frequency, the vibrations become stronger. This is resonance.

...AN ECHO?

An example of an echo is when you shout in a tunnel and you hear the noise bouncing back at you a moment later as the sound waves rebound.

WHAT OTHER ANIMALS USE ECHOLOCATION?

Toothed whales, such as porpoises, use echolocation underwater. A porpoise gives off a series of high-pitched clicking sounds and the echoes tell the porpoise where to find its prey.

HOW DO BATS LOCATE THEIR PREY?

Most bats locate their prey using echolocation. The bats send out calls, then use the echoes to locate and identify objects.

WHAT IS...

THE LARGEST LAND ANIMAL?

Elephants are the largest land animals. There are probably three species: the African bush elephant, African forest elephant, and Asian elephant. Elephants have tusks, long trunks, flapping ears, and very thick skin. After the elephant, the largest land animals are the rhinoceros, hippopotamus, and giraffe.

WHAT IS...

...A MAMMAL?	Mammals have backbones, they are hairy, and they produce milk to feed their young.
...A PRIMATE?	Primates are mammals that have large brains, hands that can form a good grip, and a tendency to walk on two legs.
...AN UNGULATE?	Ungulates are groups of mammals with hoofed feet. They include the rhinoceros, hippopotamus, and giraffe.
...A MARSUPIAL?	Marsupials are mammals whose newborns often live in a pouch on their mother's belly.
...A REPTILE?	Reptiles need to breathe air and have skin that is covered in scales.
...A RODENT?	Rodents are mammals with continuously growing incisor teeth, such as squirrels, hamsters, and mice.
...A WOMBAT?	A wombat is a small bearlike marsupial with a heavy body and short, strong legs.
...AN OKAPI?	An okapi is a relative of the giraffe that lives in the African rain forest. It does not have a long neck.
...A COYOTE?	The coyote looks similar to a wolf. It lives in North and Central America, where it hunts small mammals.
...A TASMANIAN DEVIL?	The Tasmanian devil is the largest of the flesh-eating marsupials. It is about 3 feet long.

...A DINGO?
Dingoes are Australian wild dogs. They hunt mainly sheep and rabbits.

WHY ...

... DOES A RATTLESNAKE RATTLE?

Rattlesnakes make their rattling noise to warn their enemies to stay far away. The rattle is made by a number of hard rings of skin at the end of the tail.

... DOES A KANGAROO HAVE A POUCH?

A kangaroo is less than 1 inch long when it is born. The female kangaroo has a pouch so that its young can complete its development in safety.

... DO BEAVERS BUILD DAMS?

Beavers build their homes, or lodges, in streams or rivers. But first they need to build a dam to make an area of still water, or the current would wash the lodge away.

...DO RODENTS GET LONG IN THE TOOTH?

The two sharp teeth at the front of a rodent's jaw are the ones it uses for gnawing. These get worn down, but keep on growing throughout the rodent's life.

... DO TIGERS HAVE STRIPES?

Tigers cannot run fast for long distances. Their stripes help them hide among grasses and leaves so they can get close to their prey before pouncing.

HOW MANY SPECIES...

... OF BEAR?
Eight species, ranging in size from the sun bear to huge polar bears and brown bears.

... OF DOG AND FOX?
About 35 species, including "true dogs" such as wolves, jackals, and wild dogs.

... OF LIZARD?
Probably over 4,000 species. These belong to different groups, such as geckos, iguanas, skinks, and chameleons.

... OF MONKEY?
About 260 species in two main groups. One group lives in Africa and Asia; the other lives in Central and South America.

... OF SNAKE?
About 2,700 species. They live on every continent except Antarctica.

... OF WILDCAT?
About 36 species, ranging from the tiger to the African wildcat, which is closely related to the domestic cat.

HOW MUCH DOES A KOALA EAT?
A koala eats about 1 pound of eucalyptus leaves every day, which it chews down to a fine pulp with its broad teeth.

WHICH IS THE FASTEST CAT?

The cheetah. It has been timed running at 65 miles per hour over a distance of 219 yards—more than twice as fast as humans.

HOW MUCH DO ELEPHANTS EAT?

A fully grown elephant eats 165 to 330 pounds of plant food a day. Its diet includes grass, twigs, branches, leaves, flowers, and fruits.

HOW BIG IS A BABY ELEPHANT?

A newborn baby African elephant weighs up to 265 pounds and stands up to 3 feet high.

HOW LONG ARE AN ELEPHANT'S TUSKS?

The older an elephant is, the longer its tusks. One tusk in the British Museum measures 11.5 feet.

HOW BIG IS A BABY BEAR?

Bears have tiny babies. The polar bear gives birth to cubs of only about 2 pounds, far smaller than most human babies.

HOW BIG IS A WOLF PACK?

In areas where there are plenty of large animals to catch, a pack may contain up to 30 wolves.

HOW FAST DO KANGAROOS MOVE?

A kangaroo bounds along on its strong back legs at up to 31 miles per hour. It can cover 15 yards in one giant bound.

HOW FAST DO SNAKES MOVE?

The fastest-moving snake on land is thought to be the black mamba, which lives in Africa. It can wriggle along at up to 7 miles per hour.

HOW TALL IS A GIRAFFE?

A male giraffe stands up to 18 feet tall to the tips of its horns.

WHICH IS THE BIGGEST...

... BEAR?

The polar bear is one of the largest bears. Fully grown males are over 8 feet long.

...APE?

The gorilla. A fully grown male stands up to 5.5 feet tall and weighs as much as 485 pounds.

... MONKEY?

The mandrill is the largest monkey, as it can grow to be over 3 feet long. It lives in the tropical rain forests of Central Africa.

... CAT?

Tigers are the biggest of the big cats. They can measure over 10 feet long, including the tail, and weigh 550 pounds or more.

... LIZARD?

The Komodo dragon, which lives on some Southeast Asian islands. It grows up to 10 feet long and hunts animals such as wild pigs and small deer.

... SNAKE?

The world's longest snake is the reticulated python, which grows to an amazing 33 feet long. The anaconda is heavier than the python but not quite as long.

... RODENT?

The largest rodent in the world is the capybara. It measures up to 4 feet long and weighs up to 141 pounds.

7

5

2

1

WHAT IS...

A MARINE MAMMAL?

Not all mammals live on land. Seals, sea lions, and walruses are just some of the mammals that depend on the oceans for food. Marine mammals need to breathe air, so they have to come to the water's surface regularly. They have a thick layer of blubber, or fat, which keeps them warm in the water.

HOW FAST ...

... DO FISH SWIM?

The sailfish can move at speeds of more than 68 miles per hour. Marlins and tunas are also fast swimmers.

... DO SHARKS SWIM?

Up to 50 miles per hour for short periods.

... DO SEA LIONS SWIM?

Up to 25 miles per hour.

... DO WHALES SWIM?

Blue whales can move at speeds of up to 19 miles per hour. Smaller whales, such as pilot whales and dolphins, may swim at more than 30 miles per hour.

HOW MANY ...

... TYPES OF FROG AND TOAD?

There may be as many as 4,000 species. Most live in areas with plenty of rainfall.

... TYPES OF CROCODILE?

There are 14 species of crocodile, 2 species of alligator, several species of caiman, and 1 species of gavial.

... KINDS OF SHARK?

There are over 300 different species living all over the world. They range in size from dwarf dogfish to the giant whale shark.

... GROUPS OF WHALES?

There are two groups of whales: toothed whales and whales that catch food with baleen filters.

HOW BIG IS A BABY BLUE WHALE?
A baby blue whale is about 26 feet long at birth and is the biggest baby in the animal kingdom.

HOW BIG IS A GREAT WHITE SHARK?
Great white sharks are mostly about 23 feet long, but some can grow up to 39 feet.

HOW DOES A BLUE WHALE FEED?
It opens its mouth and water full of krill flows in. The water flows out at the sides of the mouth, leaving the krill behind on baleen—bristly plates in the whale's upper jaw. The whale then swallows.

HOW DO TURTLES SWIM?
Turtles "fly" through the water with the help of their strong, paddle-shaped flippers.

3,748 lb

HOW BIG IS A WALRUS?
The largest male walruses are more than 10 feet long and weigh 3,748 pounds.

HOW CAN YOU TELL A CROCODILE FROM AN ALLIGATOR?
A crocodile's teeth stick out when its mouth is shut!

HOW CAN YOU TELL A SEAL FROM A SEA LION?
Sea lions have small ear flaps, whereas seals have only ear openings. Sea lions can bring their back flippers under the body to help them move on land, while seals drag themselves along.

WHAT IS...

... A CETACEAN?

Cetaceans are a group of marine mammals that includes whales, dolphins, and porpoises. They are highly intelligent, have large tails, and breathe air through the blowhole on the top of their head.

...A PORPOISE?

A porpoise is a small whale with a rounded head, not a beaked snout like a dolphin. They live in coastal waters in the Atlantic, Pacific, and Indian Oceans.

...A NARWHAL?

A narwhal is a whale with a single long tusk at the front of its head. The tusk is actually a tooth, which grows out from the upper jaw.

... TUSKING?

"Tusking" is when two animals, such as male narwhals, rub their tusks together.

... SPYHOPPING?

Dolphins often "spyhop," coming to the surface to look around.

...AN AMPHIBIAN?

Unlike other land animals, most amphibians lay their eggs in water. Young amphibians live and breathe in water, before transforming into air-breathing, land-living adults.

...A TADPOLE?

A tadpole is the young, or larva, of an amphibian such as a frog or newt. The amphibian egg is usually laid in water and hatches out into a small, swimming creature with a long tail.

...AN ANEMONEFISH?

Anemonefish live in sea anemones that thrive in tropical waters. They are the only fish that are immune to the poison in sea anemones.

HOW MANY ...

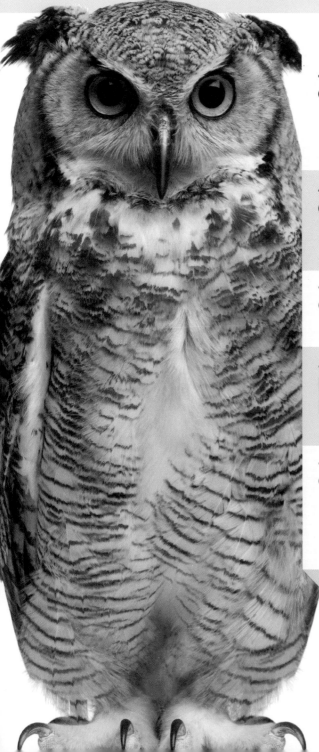

... SPECIES OF BIRD?

Around 10,000 different species. They inhabit every one of the world's ecosystems, from deserts to rain forests.

... KINDS OF GULL?

About 45. They live in all parts of the world, but there are more species north of the equator.

... KINDS OF OWL?

145 species. Owls are the only nocturnal birds of prey, usually hunting at night.

... KINDS OF BIRD OF PREY?

About 500 species, including eagles, hawks, buzzards, harriers, kites, falcons, and vultures.

... SPECIES OF PARROT?

About 350 species, all of which live in the warmer regions of the world. Parrots are among the most intelligent birds.

WHAT IS A GANNET?

Gannets are the largest seabirds in the North Atlantic Ocean, with a wingspan of up to 6.5 feet.

HOW DOES A GANNET CATCH ITS FOOD?

The gannet flies over the water looking for prey. When it sees something, it plunges into the ocean with its wings swept back, and seizes the catch in its beak.

WHAT IS A BIRD OF PREY?

Birds of prey are hunters, feeding on small animals. They have keen eyesight, sharp hearing, and strong beaks and claws.

HOW DO EAGLES KILL THEIR PREY?

An eagle drops down onto its prey, seizes it in its long talons, and crushes it to death.

WHY DOES A PELICAN HAVE A POUCH?

The pelican has a pouch to help it catch fish. Water drains from the pouch, leaving any fish behind to be swallowed.

WHAT IS A TROPICBIRD?

A tropicbird is a seabird with two very long central tail feathers. There are three species, all of which fly over tropical oceans.

WHAT DOES AN OSPREY EAT?

The osprey feeds mostly on fish. It dives to the water's surface and seizes fish in its feet.

HOW CAN OWLS HUNT AT NIGHT?

Owls have excellent sight and very sharp hearing. Special soft-edged wing feathers enable them to beat their wings very quietly.

WHICH IS THE FASTEST BIRD?

The peregrine falcon may move at about 200 miles per hour as it dives to catch other birds in the air.

IS A PUFFIN A KIND OF PENGUIN?

No, puffins belong to a family of birds called auks. They live in the northern hemisphere and are able to fly.

HOW FAST DO PENGUINS SWIM?

Penguins can swim at speeds of 8 miles per hour, but they may move even faster for short periods.

HOW MANY ...

KINDS OF PLANTS ARE THERE?

There are approximately 287,655 named species of plants, although many more are believed to exist. These range from trees, bushes, and herbs to grasses, ferns, and mosses. Most plants get their energy for growing from sunlight, using a process called photosynthesis.

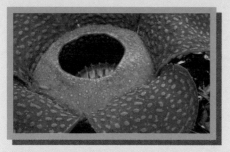

HOW DOES A FLOWER FORM SO QUICKLY?
The flower is already formed in miniature inside the bud, just waiting to open out.

WHY DO WE NEED PLANTS?
Plants reduce carbon dioxide and produce vital oxygen, which we need to survive.

HOW DO GREEN PLANTS FEED?
A pigment called chlorophyll helps to trap energy from the Sun. Plants use this energy to convert water and carbon dioxide into sugars and starch. This is called photosynthesis.

HOW DOES MISTLETOE FEED?
Mistletoe takes some nutrients from other plants by attaching itself to the branches of trees and shrubs.

HOW FAST DOES SAP FLOW THROUGH A TREE?
Sap is the fluid that transports water and food through plants. It may flow through a tree as fast as 3 feet every hour.

HOW MUCH SUGAR DO PLANTS MAKE IN A YEAR?
Scientists estimate that all the green plants in the world make more than 185 billion tons of sugar every year.

HOW DOES A VENUS FLYTRAP CATCH PREY?
It has a flattened, hinged pad at the end of each leaf, fringed with sensitive hairs. When an insect lands on the pad, the trap springs shut.

WHAT IS THE STINKIEST FLOWER?
The rafflesia in Southeast Asia mimics the aroma of rotting flesh to attract flies.

HOW DOES A PARASITIC PLANT FEED?

Parasitic plants grow into the tissues of another plant, called the host, and tap into its food and water transportation system.

WHY ARE MOST PLANTS GREEN?

Because their stems and leaves contain the green pigment chlorophyll.

WHY DO SHOOTS GROW UPWARD?

Most shoots grow upward, toward sunlight. The growing tip of the shoot can detect the direction of the light.

WHAT MAKES A SEED GROW?

To grow, a seed needs moisture, warmth, and air.

WHY DO ROOTS GROW DOWNWARD?

Roots respond to gravity by releasing chemicals that prevent growth on the lower side, thus turning the root downward.

HOW DO PLANTS TAKE IN WATER?

Plants use their roots to take in water from the ground. Water passes into the root across the cell walls of millions of tiny root hairs.

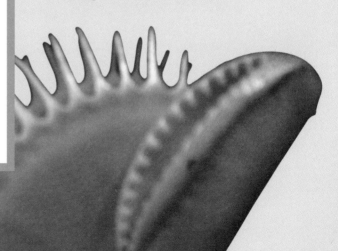

61

HOW...

...DO PLANTS RECYCLE WATER?

Plants return water to the air through transpiration. Water moves up through plants before evaporating from the stems and leaves.

...DO PLANTS MAKE SOIL MORE FERTILE?

When plants die, they decompose, releasing the chemicals in their tissues into the surrounding soil. This makes the soil more fertile.

...DO PLANTS HELP US RECLAIM LAND?

Some grasses can be planted on coastal dunes to keep sand from blowing away. Other plants tolerate toxic substances and gradually improve the quality of soil.

...DO FORESTS HELP IMPROVE THE AIR?

Forests release huge quantities of water vapor and oxygen into the atmosphere. Plants also absorb carbon dioxide.

...ARE PLANTS USED TO CLEAN UP SEWAGE?

Sewage works use tiny algae and other microscopic organisms in their filter beds. These feed on pollutants and help to clean the water.

...CAN PLANTS BE USED TO HELP STOP EROSION?

Erosion is when soil is removed by natural forces such as wind and water. Plants can reduce this because their roots trap loose soil and keep it from being blown or washed away.

HOW LONG HAVE PEOPLE BEEN USING PLANTS AS MEDICINE?

For at least 100,000 years. Today, scientists are still researching the valuable healing properties of plants for use in conventional medicines.

WHICH COUNTRIES USE THE MOST HERBAL REMEDIES?

In China and India, herbal remedies are used more than any other kind of medicine.

CAN PLANTS HELP FIGHT CANCER?

Several plants are effective against cancer tumors. Vincristine—an extract of the rosy periwinkle—is very effective against some types of leukemia.

CAN WILLOWS HELP PAIN?

Willow twigs were once chewed to give pain relief. A compound similar to the drug aspirin was once extracted from willows and the herb meadowsweet.

WHICH PLANTS AID DIGESTION?

Many plants, including the herbs and spices used in cooking, help digestion. In Europe, the bitter extract of wild gentians provides a good remedy for digestive problems.

WHAT IS...

... GINSENG?	Ginseng is related to ivy. It is claimed to help many conditions, including heart problems and headaches.
... JOJOBA?	Jojoba is a bush found in Mexico. The fruits have an oily wax used in inks, body lotions, and shampoos.
... QUININE?	Quinine, from the bark of the quinine tree, can cure or prevent malaria.
... LUNGWORT?	Lungwort is an herb with spotted leaves that are said to look like lungs. Some people use it to treat asthma.

HOW IS CHOCOLATE MADE?

The cacao tree develops fruits, called pods, on the sides of its trunk. Each pod contains 20 to 60 seeds—the cocoa "beans." The beans must be fermented, roasted, and ground before they become cocoa powder, which is used to make chocolate.

WHAT DO PEOPLE DRINK THE MOST?

After water, tea is the world's most consumed drink.

HOW IS TEA MADE?

Tea comes from the leaves of a camellia grown in India, Sri Lanka, Indonesia, Japan, and China. The young leaf tips are harvested, dried, and crushed to make tea.

WHERE DOES COFFEE COME FROM?

Coffee comes from the berries of the coffee plant. Ripe berries are harvested, then dried. The hard stones inside are the coffee "beans," which are then often roasted.

WHAT TREES GIVE US A SWEET, SUGARY SYRUP?

The sugar maple has a sweet sap, harvested to make maple syrup.

WHAT IS THE AMAZON COW TREE?

The Amazon cow tree is a tropical fig. It produces a milklike sap, which can be drunk just like cow's milk.

WHICH PLANTS GIVE US OIL?

The olive plant, sunflower, corn, soybean, peanut, oilseed rape, sesame, and African oil palm.

WHAT IS BREADFRUIT?

Breadfruit is a tree native to the Malay Archipelago. It has large edible fruits that are eaten as a vegetable.

WHAT IS...

AN ECOSYSTEM?

An ecosystem is a community of plants and animals that live in the same area or environment. The world has many different ecosystems, each with its own climate, soil, and living things. Some ecosystems are small, such as ponds or coral reefs. Other ecosystems, including forests and deserts, are much larger. Many ecosystems need to be protected because growing human populations are putting them under threat.

WHAT IS A DESERT?

A desert is an area that receives very little rain and so is unable to support much plant growth. Although many deserts are in hot regions, some of the world's deserts can be extremely cold.

WHY ARE SOME DESERTS EXPANDING?

The Sahara grows larger each year, partly because the climate is getting gradually warmer, but mainly because the plant life on the edges of the desert has been destroyed by grazing animals.

WHICH IS THE DRIEST DESERT?

The Sahara is one of the driest deserts. The Atacama Desert in Chile is also very dry, with years often passing between rainfalls.

WHAT ARE LIVING STONES?

Living stones are desert plants from southern Africa. They grow low down on the desert's surface, looking like small pebbles or rocks.

WHAT IS...

...A RAIN SHADOW?
A rain shadow is a dry region of land that lies close to a mountain range. The mountains block rain-bringing clouds, casting a "shadow" of dryness.

...AN OASIS?
An oasis is a place in the desert where water is in plentiful supply, such as at a pool fed by a spring.

...A JOSHUA TREE?
The Joshua tree grows in the Mojave Desert, U.S. Each of its leaves can survive for up to 20 years.

...A PRICKLY PEAR?
It is a type of cactus. The fruits of prickly pears can be eaten, as long as their small spines are removed.

...A YUCCA PLANT?
Yucca plants are succulents—they are adapted to very dry conditions and store water in their leaves.

WHAT ARE ... GRASSLANDS AND WETLANDS?

Grassland develops in temperate regions—lying between the polar areas and the tropics—that have warm summers and cold winters, and where there is not enough rainfall for trees and woods to grow.

WHAT NAMES ARE GIVEN TO GRASSLANDS?

The Asian grasslands are called the steppes, and the North American grasslands are the prairies. In Argentina, they are called pampas, and in southern Africa, the veld.

WHAT ARE GRASSLANDS USED FOR?

Because the soils are so fertile, much grassland has been plowed and planted with crops. Grasslands are also used for grazing herds of animals, such as cows.

WETLANDS include swamps, bogs, and marshes. Wetland plants are adapted to living in water-soaked soil. Cattails, water lilies, and mangroves are just some of the common wetland species.

WHAT FOOD PLANTS COME FROM WETLANDS?

The most important wetland crop is rice. It grows best in flooded fields called paddies.

HOW ARE WETLANDS DAMAGED?

When soil is drained, or too much water is pumped from the land nearby, wetlands suffer as the water table is lowered. They are also easily damaged by pollution: Chemicals released from factories find their way into nearby streams.

67

WHAT ARE CONIFEROUS FORESTS?

Coniferous forests contain coniferous trees such as pines and firs. These are evergreen trees, which do not lose their leaves in winter.

WHICH IS THE WORLD'S HIGHEST MOUNTAIN RANGE? The

Himalayas, in Asia. It contains 96 of the world's 109 peaks that are more than 24,000 feet above sea level.

HOW COLD IS MOUNTAIN AIR?

As you climb a mountain, the air temperature falls about 1.8°F for every 500 feet you ascend in height.

WHICH IS THE WORLD'S HIGHEST MOUNTAIN?

At 29,029 feet to the summit, Mount Everest, in the Himalayas, is the world's highest mountain.

WHAT IS THE TREE LINE?

Trees cannot grow all the way up a mountain and the highest level for them is known as the tree line.

WHY IS IT COLDER IN THE MOUNTAINS?

The Sun heats the ground and this heat is trapped by the Earth's atmosphere. As you go up a mountain, and rise above the zone in which the heat is held, the atmosphere becomes thinner and the air gets colder.

WHY IS IT DAMAGING TO CUT DOWN MOUNTAIN FORESTS?

Tree roots anchor the soil, keeping it from being washed away by rain running down the slopes. Without trees, dangerous landslides can occur.

HOW DOES MOUNTAIN PLANT LIFE REFLECT HARSH CONDITIONS?

Conditions get harsher the higher you go up a mountain. Fir or pine forest on the upper slopes gives way to shrubs then grassland, followed by snow and rock.

WHY ARE ALPINE PLANTS POPULAR IN GARDENS?

Alpine plants are popular because they have bright flowers and tend to grow well in poor conditions.

WHY DO DIFFERENT PLANTS GROW ON DIFFERENT SIDES OF A MOUNTAIN?

Because on the south side (or north side in the southern hemisphere), there is more sunshine and conditions are warmer, while on the other side, the snow stays on the ground much longer.

HOW...

... DO PLANTS SURVIVE THE COLD?

Some grow close to the ground, keeping out of the wind. Others have thick, waxy, or hairy leaves to help insulate them from the cold.

... DO PLANTS SURVIVE SNOW AND ICE?

Few plants can survive being frozen, but many thrive under snow. The snow acts like a blanket.

... DO MOUNTAIN PLANTS ATTRACT POLLINATORS?

Many mountain plants have large, colorful flowers to attract insects. Some track the Sun to warm their flowers, which encourages insects to sunbathe there.

... DO SOME MOUNTAIN PLANTS REPRODUCE WITHOUT FLOWERS?

Some grasses grow miniature plants where the flowers should be. These drop off and grow into new plants.

... DO PLANT-EATING ANIMALS FIND FOOD IN THE MOUNTAINS?

Many mountain mammals burrow under the snow and continue to feed on mountain plants. Others store fat in their bodies and hibernate during the winter.

WHERE ARE THE RAIN FORESTS?

The world's largest rain forest is around Brazil's Amazon River and the foothills of the Andes Mountains. The world's main areas of tropical rain forest are in South and Central America, West and Central Africa, Southeast Asia, and north Australia.

WHY DO WE NEED RAIN FORESTS?

Rain forests help preserve the planet's atmosphere by releasing huge quantities of water vapor and oxygen, and absorbing carbon dioxide.

WHAT DO WE GET FROM RAIN FORESTS?

We get many things from rain forests, including timber, Brazil nuts, fruit, rubber, rattan, cosmetics, and medicines.

HOW FAST ARE RAIN FORESTS BEING DESTROYED?

Every year, an area of rain forest the size of the state of Wisconsin is lost.

HOW MUCH RAIN FALLS IN THE RAIN FOREST?

In many tropical rain forests, the rainfall is more than 6.5 feet per year.

ARE RAIN FORESTS VITAL?

Yes! Rain forests are home to two-thirds of the world's animal and plant species. And without rain forests to regulate the Earth's atmosphere, climate change would speed up.

WHY ARE RAIN FORESTS BEING CUT DOWN?

Many rain forests are destroyed so the land can be used for crops, or for grazing. Tropical forest soils are fertile and many crops can be grown after the trees have been felled.

HOW MANY LAYERS MAKE UP A RAIN FOREST?

The rain forest is in four basic layers. At the top are the very tallest trees. Below is the canopy, a dense cover of foliage. The understory is a layer of shrubs, while the forest floor below is relatively bare.

HOW TALL ARE THE BIGGEST RAIN FOREST TREES?

The main canopy of the rain forest develops at around 100 feet, with occasional taller trees rising to 165 feet or more.

WHAT STOPS THE TALL TREES FROM BEING BLOWN OVER?

Many of the taller forest trees have special supporting flanges near the base of their trunks, called stilts or buttresses.

HOW DO WE...

KNOW ABOUT WHAT WAS HERE BEFORE US?

Humans have only been on the Earth for about 100,000 years. But scientists can form a picture of our planet's history before humans existed by studying the Earth's rocks and fossils. We have discovered when the earliest life-forms emerged and what the first animals looked like.

HOW IS THE EARTH'S HISTORY DIVIDED?

Scientists divide the last 590 million years into three eras: the Paleozoic (meaning old life), Mesozoic (middle life), and Cenozoic (new life). Earth's history before the Paleozoic era is divided into three eons: the Hadean, Archean, and Proterozoic.

WHY IS THE CAMBRIAN PERIOD IMPORTANT?

Before the Cambrian period, most living creatures were soft-bodied and left few fossils. During the Cambrian period, many creatures had hard parts, which were preserved as fossils in layers of rock.

WHEN DID PLANTS START TO GROW ON LAND?

The first land plants appeared in the Silurian period. Plants produced oxygen and provided food for the first land animals.

WHY WASN'T THERE LIFE ON EARTH RIGHT AWAY?

Life did not exist for the first 400–800 million years because the Earth's surface was probably molten.

WHAT DID EARLY ANIMALS LOOK LIKE?

By around 500 million years ago, bacteria in the oceans had evolved into the earliest fish with funnel-like sucking mouths.

WHAT WERE THE FIRST ANIMALS WITH BACKBONES?

Jawless fish were the first animals with backbones. They appeared during the Ordovician period.

WHAT ARE STROMATOLITES?

About 3,800 million years ago, primitive life-forms lived in the oceans. They formed deposits called stromatolites.

3,500 MILLION YEARS BC

500 MILLION YEARS BC

WHAT WERE THE FIRST LAND ANIMALS?

Amphibians. They first developed in the Devonian period from fish whose fins had evolved into limbs.

WHEN DID MAMMALS FIRST APPEAR?

Mammals lived on Earth from at least the start of the Jurassic period. But they did not become common until after the extinction of the dinosaurs.

WHEN DID DINOSAURS DIE OUT?

At the end of the Cretaceous period, 65 million years ago.

WHAT IS EVOLUTION?

Evolution is the process of how life-forms change over the course of generations. When an animal develops a successful new feature, it is passed down to future generations.

WHAT ARE PERIODS AND EPOCHS?

The geological eras are subdivided into periods. Periods are then divided into epochs.

WHY DID DINOSAURS BECOME EXTINCT?

Many experts believe an enormous asteroid struck the Earth. The impact threw up a huge cloud of dust, which blocked sunlight for a long time. Land plants died and the dinosaurs starved to death.

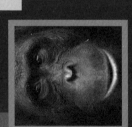

WHEN DID PEOPLE FIRST LIVE ON EARTH?

Hominids (apelike creatures that walked upright) first appeared on Earth over 4 million years ago.

WHO WERE THE NEANDERTHALS?

Neanderthals were relatives of modern humans that disappeared 24,000 years ago.

65 MILLION YEARS **BC**

24,000 YEARS **BC**

WHAT ARE FOSSILS?

Fossils are the impressions of ancient life preserved in rocks. When creatures die, their remains are often slowly buried in sand or soil. Their soft parts usually rot, but the hard parts—such as bones, teeth, and shells—can be preserved as minerals or molds in the rock.

WHAT CAN SCIENTISTS LEARN FROM DINOSAUR FOOTPRINTS?

Dinosaur tracks can tell scientists about the length of the animal's legs and the speed at which it was moving.

HOW ARE FOSSILS TURNED TO STONE?

When tree trunks or bones are buried, minerals deposited from water sometimes replace the original material. The wood or bone is then petrified, or turned to stone.

WHAT ARE TRACE FOSSILS?

Trace fossils give information about animals that lived in ancient times. Examples include animal burrows and footprints.

WHAT ARE THE THREE MAIN KINDS OF ROCK?

There are igneous, sedimentary, and metamorphic rocks. Igneous rocks, such as basalts and granites, are formed from cooled magma. Many sedimentary rocks are made from worn fragments of other rocks. For example, sandstone is formed from sand. Sand consists mainly of quartz, a mineral found in granite. Metamorphic rocks are changed by heat and pressure. For example, great heat turns limestone into marble.

GOLD NUGGETS

GRANITE

WHAT ARE MINERALS?

Minerals are solids that are formed naturally in the Earth. A common mineral is quartz. Like all minerals, it has a crystal structure—a symmetrical shape like that of a snowflake. Rocks are made of a mixture of minerals. Sandstone and limestone both contain quartz.

DIAMONDS

MARBLE

WHAT IS THE EARTH'S SURFACE MADE FROM?

The Earth's hard outer layers are divided into large blocks called plates, which float on a partly molten layer of rock. Currents in the molten rock slowly move the plates around.

HOW MANY PLATES COVER THE EARTH?
There are seven major and seven minor plates.

WHAT HAPPENS WHEN PLATES COLLIDE?
If plates collide beneath an ocean, one plate is pulled beneath the other and is melted and recycled. On land, when continents collide, their edges are squeezed up into new mountain ranges.

HOW FAST DO PLATES MOVE?
Plates move, on average, between 1.5 and 3 inches a year.

CAN PLATES MOVE SIDEWAYS?
Yes. Plates can move apart, push against each other, or move sideways along huge cracks in the ground.

HOW DEEP ARE PLATES?
Their exact thickness is uncertain but the larger plates could be up to 90 miles in places.

WHEN DID THE HIMALAYAS FORM?
They started to form when plates collided about 50 million years ago.

WHAT IS THE EARTH'S MANTLE?
The mantle is a partly molten rocky shell that surrounds the Earth's core and makes up 70% of the Earth's volume.

HAS EARTH ALWAYS LOOKED THE SAME?

No. If aliens had visited Earth 200 million years ago, they would have seen one huge continent surrounded by one ocean.

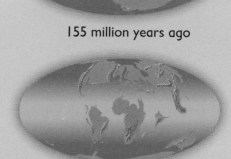

220 million years ago

155 million years ago

60 million years ago

WHAT IS CONTINENTAL DRIFT?

The continents lie on different plates, which constantly move. This movement is called continental drift.

HOW IS CONTINENTAL DRIFT MEASURED?

Around the world, observation stations measure the time taken for lasers to bounce back from satellites. This provides details of where the continents are and how they are moving.

ARE THE CONTINENTS STILL MOVING?

Yes. Africa is moving northward into Europe at the rate of fractions of an inch a year. The Americas are moving farther from Africa.

WHO FIRST SUGGESTED THE IDEA OF CONTINENTAL DRIFT?

F.B. Taylor and Alfred Wegener both suggested the idea in the early 1900s.

HAVE FOSSILS HELPED TO PROVE CONTINENTAL DRIFT?

Fossils of animals that could not have swum across oceans have been found on different continents. This suggests that animals could once walk from one continent to another.

HOW WAS HAWAII FORMED?

The Hawaiian islands were created as the Pacific Plate passed over a hot spot in the mantle. A series of new volcanoes was punched up through the surface. Each of the Hawaiian islands has a volcano.

WHAT IS ...
WEATHERING?

There are two forms of weathering. Physical weathering is the breakdown of rocks through contact with atmospheric conditions such as heat, water, ice, and pressure. Chemical weathering is caused by chemicals naturally occurring in the atmosphere.

Weathering is the slow process that causes rocks and other materials to wear away. Things that contribute to weathering include water, the sun, frost, plants, and animals. Weathering can create some of the Earth's most beautiful natural features.

WHY DO WATERFALLS OCCUR?

Waterfalls can occur when rivers cross hard rocks. When softer rocks downstream are worn away, the hard rocks form a ledge over which the river plunges in a waterfall.

WHERE DO RIVERS START?

Some rivers start at springs, where groundwater reaches the surface. Others start at the ends of melting glaciers or are the outlets of lakes.

HOW DO RIVERS WEAR AWAY THE LAND?

Young rivers push loose rocks down steep slopes. The rocks rub against riverbeds and deepen valleys. The rocks also rub against each other and break into finer pieces.

HOW DO CANYONS FORM?

A fast-moving river carrying large rocks can slowly wear away the riverbed. Over time, the river may erode a steep canyon.

WHAT IS AN OXBOW LAKE?

Sometimes slow-flowing rivers change course. Cutoff bends become oxbow lakes, with a distinctive curved shape.

WHAT ARE DELTAS?

Deltas are areas of sediments, made up of sand, mud, and silt, that pile up around the mouths of some rivers.

WHAT ARE TRIBUTARY RIVERS?

Tributary rivers are rivers that flow into a main river.

HOW DOES WATER WEATHER ROCKS?

Water dissolves rock salt. It also reacts with some types of the hard rock granite, turning minerals in the rock into a clay called kaolin.

WHAT ARE ARCHES AND STACKS?

Waves hollow out arches in rocky headlands, which eventually collapse into stacks.

HOW CAN PEOPLE SLOW DOWN WAVE EROSION?

On many beaches, structures are built at right angles to the shore. These breakwaters slow down the movement of sand by waves and currents.

WHAT IS A BLOWHOLE?

It is a hole in the rock above a sea cave. When waves enter the cave's mouth, they travel up into the blowhole, sometimes causing blasts of water.

WHAT IS A BAYMOUTH BAR?

Some spits join one headland to another. They are called baymouth bars, because they can cut off bays from the sea, turning them into enclosed lagoons.

WHAT ARE SPITS?

In places where the coasts change direction, sand and pebbles pile up in narrow ridges called spits.

DOES THE SEA WEAR AWAY THE LAND?

Waves wear away soft rocks to form bays, while harder rocks on either side form headlands.

HOW QUICKLY IS THE LAND WORN AWAY?

An average of 1.5 inches is worn away in 100 years. Over millions of years, mountains can be worn down to plains.

HOW ARE NATURAL WONDERS MADE?

Many of the Earth's beautiful features were created by weathering, erosion, and the work of rivers, sea, and ice.

WHERE IS...

...THE LONGEST BEACH?	Cox's Bazar Beach in Bangladesh is the longest sandy sea beach at 78 miles.
... THE LARGEST CANYON?	The Grand Canyon in the United States. It is 277 miles long and 1 mile deep.
... THE TALLEST STALAGMITE?	It may be in the cave of San Martin Infierno in Cuba, measuring 220 feet.
...THE GREAT PEBBLE?	Ayers Rock in central Australia is also known as Uluru, meaning "great pebble."
...THE GREAT BARRIER REEF?	It lies off the northeast coast of Australia and is about 1,240 miles long.
... "SMOKE THAT THUNDERS?"	This is the local name of the beautiful Victoria Falls on the Zambezi River in Africa.

WHERE ARE THE NEEDLES?

The Needles are a row of chalk stacks, eroded by waves, that lie off the Isle of Wight in southern England.

WHAT ARE HOODOOS?

Hoodoos can be seen at Bryce Canyon, in Utah. These rock needles are formed by water, wind, and ice erosion.

WHERE IS THE MATTERHORN?

The Matterhorn is a magnificent mountain on Switzerland's border with Italy.

HOW TALL IS THE MATTERHORN?

The Matterhorn reaches a height of 14,692 feet above sea level.

WHAT IS THE GREAT BARRIER REEF? It is the world's longest group of coral reefs and islands.

IS THERE A LAKE UNDER ANTARCTICA? Yes. Scientists have found a lake, about the size of Lake Ontario in North America, hidden under Antarctica.

HOW ARE NATURAL WONDERS PROTECTED? In 1872, the world's first national park was founded at Yellowstone in the northwestern United States. Since then, national parks have been founded around the world to protect natural wonders.

WHICH JAPANESE WONDER ATTRACTS PILGRIMS? Mount Fuji in Japan is regarded as a sacred mountain by many people, who make long pilgrimages to the top.

WHAT IS GLOBAL WARMING?

It is a rise in average worldwide temperatures. This is partly caused by activities such as deforestation and the burning of fossil fuels, such as coal. These activities release greenhouse gases, such as the carbon dioxide stored in trees. These gases trap heat in the Earth's atmosphere. Global warming is likely to cause changes in rainfall patterns, causing floods in some areas and droughts in others.

WHAT IS DEFORESTATION?

When trees are cut down without new trees being planted, deforestation takes place. Today, the tropical rain forests are particularly affected by deforestation. These forests contain more than half of the world's species—many are threatened with extinction.

WHAT IS AIR POLLUTION?

Air pollution occurs when gases such as carbon dioxide are emitted into the air by factories, homes, and offices. Vehicles also cause air pollution, which produces city smogs, acid rain, and global warming.

WHAT IS DESERTIFICATION?

Desertification is when fertile land is turned into desert. This is caused by cutting down trees, overgrazing grassland, or by natural climate changes.

WILL GLOBAL WARMING AFFECT ANY ISLAND NATIONS?

If global warming melts the world's ice, then sea levels will rise. Low-lying countries such as the Maldives and Kiribati could vanish under the waves.

WHAT IS SOIL EROSION?

Soil erosion occurs when people cut down trees and farm the land. Soil erosion on land made bare by people is a much faster process than natural erosion.

WHAT POLLUTES RIVERS?

Pollution in rivers includes garbage, chemicals, and sewage.

CAN DESERTS BE FARMED?

Yes. In the U.S. and other countries, barren deserts are watered from wells that tap groundwater, or water piped from faraway areas.

MUSCLES ARE IN THE HUMAN BODY?

There are about 650 muscles in the human body. They work together to move your bones, as well as giving your body its shape. Most actions—including walking, swimming, and smiling—involve dozens of muscles. Different kinds of muscles make the heart beat and move food through the intestines.

WHAT DOES SKIN DO?

Skin stops the moisture inside the body from getting out and stops germs getting in. Tiny particles in the skin also help to shield your body from the Sun's harmful rays.

WHAT IS A FINGERPRINT?

A fingerprint is made by thin ridges of skin on the tip of each finger and thumb. The ridges form a pattern of lines, loops, or whorls.

ARE FINGERPRINTS UNIQUE?

Yes! Every person's fingerprint is different. Fingerprints are often used for identification.

WHY DO WE HAVE NAILS?

Nails protect our fingers and toes as well as help us to grasp objects.

HOW FAST DO NAILS GROW?

A fingernail grows about 0.04 inches every week.

WHY DOES HAIR FALL OUT?

No hair lasts more than about six years. Every day you lose about 60 hairs.

WHY DOES SKIN HAVE PORES?

Skin has tiny holes, called pores, to let out sweat when you are too hot.

WHAT GIVES HAIR ITS COLOR?

Hair color depends on a pigment called melanin. Lighter melanin causes blond or red hair. Darker melanin causes brown or black hair.

HOW FAST DO NERVES ACT?

A nerve signal travels at about 3 feet per second in the slowest nerves and more than 328 feet per second in the fastest.

HOW DOES A NERVE WORK?

A chain of nerve cells carries a signal to or from the brain. The electrical impulse is received by the nerve endings and sent from one nerve cell to the next.

WHAT ARE THE BODY'S FIVE MAIN SENSES?

The five main senses are seeing, hearing, smelling, tasting, and touching.

HOW DOES TOUCH WORK?

Different kinds of sense receptors in the skin react to touch, heat, cold, and pain. The brain puts together all the different messages to tell you if something is shiny, wet, cold, and many other things.

CAN BLIND PEOPLE USE TOUCH TO READ?

Yes. Blind people can run their fingertips over Braille—a pattern of raised dots that represent different letters.

HOW DOES SMELL WORK?

A smell is made by tiny particles in the air. When you breathe in, these particles dissolve in mucus in the nose. Smell receptors in the nose respond to this and send a message to the brain.

HOW DO YOU DETECT TASTE?

As you chew, tiny particles of food dissolve in saliva and trickle down to the taste buds on the tongue. The taste receptors react and send messages to the brain.

WHAT DOES THE SKULL DO?

The skull is a hard covering of bone that protects the brain like a helmet. All the bones of the skull except the lower jaw are fused together to make them stronger.

HOW MANY BONES DO WE HAVE?

An adult has about 206 bones.
All the bones together are called the skeleton.

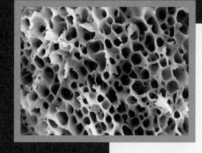

WHAT IS INSIDE A BONE?

Inside the larger bones is a crisscross honeycomb. Blood vessels weave in and out of the bone, keeping the cells alive.

WHAT IS A JOINT?

Where two bones meet, their ends are shaped to make different kinds of joints. The knee is a hinge joint that lets the lower leg move only backward and forward. The hip is a ball and socket joint that allows you to move your thigh in a circle.

HOW DO MUSCLES WORK?

Muscles work by contracting. Each muscle is connected to at least two bones. When they contract, muscles get shorter and thicker, so they pull the bones together, causing the body to move.

WHICH IS THE BIGGEST MUSCLE?

The biggest muscle is the gluteus maximus in the buttock. You can use it to straighten your leg when you stand up and it makes a comfortable cushion to sit on.

WHY DO MUSCLES WORK IN PAIRS?

Because muscles cannot push, they can only pull. For example, to bend your elbow, you tighten the biceps muscle at the front of your upper arm. To straighten the elbow again, you relax the biceps and tighten the triceps muscle at the back of your upper arm.

HOW DO YOU SEE SOMETHING?

You see an object when light bounces off it and enters your eyes. The black circle in the middle of the eye is called the pupil. Light passes through the pupil and is focused by the lens onto the retina at the back of the eye. The retina sends signals to the brain.

HOW BIG IS AN EYEBALL?

An adult eyeball is about the size of a golf ball, but most of the eyeball is hidden inside your head.

WHY DO YOU HAVE TWO EYES?

Two eyes help you to judge how far away something is. Each eye gets a slightly different picture, which the brain combines into a single 3D picture.

HOW DO YOU HEAR?

Sound reaches your ears as vibrations in the air. The vibrations travel to the eardrum, which makes the bones in the middle ear vibrate, too. These pass the vibrations to the fluid around the cochlea in the inner ear. Nerve endings in the cochlea send signals to the brain.

WHY DO YOUR EARS POP?

When the air inside and outside the eardrum are at different pressures, you may go a bit deaf. Your ears "pop" when the pressures become equal.

WHY DO YOU GET DIZZY?

You feel dizzy when fluid in the semicircular canals of your ears is still moving, even though you may be standing still.

WHAT HAPPENS WHEN YOU BREATHE?

When you breathe in, you pull air through the mouth or nose into the windpipe and down to the lungs. Oxygen in the air is passed into the blood, then carried to all parts of the body.

HOW DO YOU TALK?

When you breathe out, the air passes over the vocal cords in the voice box, or larynx, in the neck. When the cords vibrate, they make a sound. Changing the shape of your lips and tongue makes different sounds.

HOW LONG CAN YOU HOLD YOUR BREATH?

You can probably hold your breath for about a minute.

WHY...

... DO YOU COUGH?	To clear the air passages between your nose and lungs from mucus, dust, or other particles.
... DOES RUNNING MAKE YOU PUFF?	Because your muscles are working hard and need extra oxygen.
... DO YOU SWEAT WHEN YOU ARE HOT?	To help cool the body. The salty liquid (sweat) takes heat from the body as it evaporates.
... IS BLOOD RED?	Blood gets its color from billions of red blood cells, which contain hemoglobin.
... IS URINE YELLOW?	Because it contains traces of waste bile, which makes it yellowish.

WHAT DOES THE HEART DO?

The heart's job is to pump blood to the lungs and then all around the body. The right side of the heart pumps blood to the lungs. The left side takes blood filled with oxygen from the lungs and pumps it around the body.

WHAT DO WHITE BLOOD CELLS DO?

They surround and destroy germs and other intruders that get into the blood.

WHAT DOES THE LIVER DO?

The intestines pass digested food to the liver, where some nutrients may be released into the blood and the rest stored to be used later. The liver also processes poisons in the blood and changes unwanted proteins into urea.

WHAT IS...

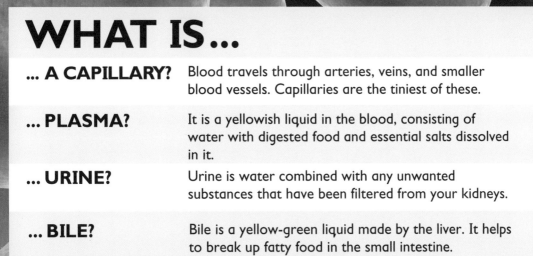

... A CAPILLARY?	Blood travels through arteries, veins, and smaller blood vessels. Capillaries are the tiniest of these.
... PLASMA?	It is a yellowish liquid in the blood, consisting of water with digested food and essential salts dissolved in it.
... URINE?	Urine is water combined with any unwanted substances that have been filtered from your kidneys.
... BILE?	Bile is a yellow-green liquid made by the liver. It helps to break up fatty food in the small intestine.

INDEX

A

Aboriginals 27, 33
absolute zero 44
acceleration 42
acid rain 82
Africa 50, 52, 67, 70, 76
air pollution 82
air pressure 38
algae 62
alligators 54, 55
alpine plants 69
Althing 20
Amazon cow tree 64
amino acids 16
amphibians 56, 73
anacondas 52
Andromeda Galaxy 16
anemonefish 56
animals 46, 47–58, 69, 72, 73, 74
Antarctica 44, 81
Antares 15
apes 52
Aphrodite 31
arches 79
artworks 27, 28
Asia 18, 32, 50, 67, 70
asteroids 5, 73
asthma 63
astronomers 11, 15
Atacama Desert 66
Athens 21
atmosphere 8, 10, 45, 62, 68, 70, 77, 82
atomic mass 37
atomic numbers 37
atoms 12, 37, 38, 39, 40, 43, 44
Australia 27, 33, 70, 80
Ayers Rock 80
Aztecs 32

B

bacteria 72
Bangladesh 80
batik 25
bats 46
batteries 39, 43
baymouth bars 79
bays 79
beaches 80
bears 50, 51, 52
beavers 49
Beijing opera 27
Big Bang 12, 13
Big Crunch 16
bile 88, 89
binaries 14
birds 57–58
birds of prey 57, 58
birth of a star 15
black mambas 51
blood 88, 89
blowholes 79
blubber 53
blue whales 54, 55
body language 22
bogs 67
bones 86
borders 18
Boyle's Law 39
Braille 85
brains 48, 85, 86, 87
breadfruit 64
breakwaters 79
breathing 88
Britain 25, 26, 31, 34, 81
Buddhism 23
Burns, Robert 27

C

cacao trees 64
cacti 66
caimans 54
calendar months 6
Cambodia 26
Cambrian Period 72
camellias 64
cancer 63
canyons 78, 80
capillaries 89
capital cities 18, 20
capybaras 52
carbon 12, 16, 38
carbon chains 38
carbon dioxide 39, 60, 62, 70, 82
Caribbean 18, 27
Carnival 25, 27
cats 50, 52
cells 16, 38, 85, 86, 88, 89
central heating 31
centurions 31
cetaceans 56
chameleons 50
cheese 27
cheetahs 50
chemical reactions 39, 44
child labor 34
Children's Day 26
China 22, 27, 62, 64
Chinese New Year 28
chlorophyll 60, 61
chocolate 64
Christianity 23, 24
Christmas 24
cities 18, 20
climate change 66, 70, 82
clogs 26
clouds 39, 43
clusters 13, 14
Cockcroft, John 40
coffee 64
colliders 13
comets 5
communication 22

compounds 38
computers 43
condensation 39
conduction 38, 43
coniferous forests 68
constellations 14
continental drift 76
continents 18, 75, 76
Cook, James 33
coral reefs 81
corona 8
coughing 88
counties 18
countries 17–21
cows 67
coyotes 48
Crick, Francis 40
crocodiles 54, 55
Crusades 32
culture 25–28
Curie, Marie 40
currencies 19

D

dams 49
dancing 25, 26, 28
days 6
deforestation 70, 82
deltas 78
democracies 19
Denmark 20
departments 18
dependent nations 18
desertification 82
deserts 66, 82
digestion 63, 89
dingoes 48
dinosaurs 73, 74
dissolving 39
Diwali 24
dizziness 87
DNA 38, 40
dogs 48, 50
dolphins 54, 56
dragon dance 28
drama 25, 28
Dreamtime 27
droughts 82
drums 27, 28

E

eagles 57, 58
earliest life-forms 71, 72
ears 87
Earth 6, 7, 8, 9, 16, 71–82
echoes 46
echolocation 46
eclipses 8, 9
ecosystems 65–70
Egypt, ancient 29–30
electric currents 38, 39, 43
electrical charge 37, 43
electricity 38, 41, 43
electrolysis 38
electron shells 37
electrons 37, 38, 39, 43
elements 35, 37, 38, 40
elephants 47, 51
elliptical galaxies 13
empires 18, 31, 32
energy 8, 12, 13, 39, 41, 42,
    44, 60
English language 22
erosion 62, 78, 79, 80, 82
Esperanto 22
Europe 76
evaporation 36, 62, 88
evening star 10
evolution 73
expansion of the Universe 16
extinction 82
eyeballs 87
eyes 87

F

factories 34, 67, 82
farming 67, 70, 82
fashion 28
fasting 24
Feria 26
festivals 24, 25, 27, 28
fiberoptic cables 45
Fifth of November 26
fingerprints 84
fire 39, 44
fish 54, 72, 73
five Ks 24
flags 20

floods 82
flowers 60
food 26, 27, 67
forces 12, 38, 42
forests 62, 68, 70, 82
fossil fuels 41, 82
fossils 71, 72, 74, 76
foxes 50
Franklin, Rosalind 40
frequencies 46
frogs 54, 56
fulcrum 42

G

galaxies 5, 11, 12, 13, 16
Gambia 28
gannets 58
gases 8, 12, 15, 36, 37, 39, 82
gavials 54
geckos 50
Geiger counters 40
Genghis Khan 32
gentians 63
geological eras, periods
    and epochs 73
germs 84, 89
ginseng 63
giraffes 47, 48, 51
glaciers 78
global warming 66, 82
gods and goddesses 21, 24,
    28, 31
gorillas 52
governments 18
Grand Canyon 80
granite 74, 78
grasslands 33, 67, 69
gravity 9, 11, 12, 15, 42
Great Barrier Reef 80, 81
Great Exhibition 34
Great Plains 33
Great Stink 34
great white sharks 55
Greece, ancient 31
greenhouse gases 82
groundwater 78, 82
gulls 57

H

Hadrian's Wall 31
haggis 27
hair 43, 84
hair color 84
haka 26
hamsters 48
Hanukkah 24
Hawaiian islands 76
headlands 79
heads of state 19
hearing 87
heart 89
heat 8, 10, 12, 15, 38, 39,
   41, 44
helium 12, 13
herbal remedies 62
Himalayas 68, 75
Hinduism 23, 24
hippos 47, 48
history 29–34
holy books 23
hominids 73
hoodoos 81
human body 83–89
humans, early 73
hydrogen 10, 12, 13, 35, 37, 40

I

ice and snow 5, 69, 82
Iceland 20
igneous rocks 74
iguanas 50
Incas 32
independent nations 18
India 24, 28, 62, 64
Industrial Revolution 34
inertia 42
inflation 13
intestines 89
ions 38, 39
Ireland 26
iron 12
irregular galaxies 13
Islam 23, 24, 32
islands 18, 76

J

jackals 50
Japan 20, 24, 25, 64, 81
Jerusalem 24, 32
Jesus Christ 24
joints 86
jojoba 63
Joshua trees 66
Judaism 23, 24
Jupiter 7, 10

K

kabuki 25
kangaroos 49, 51
kaolin 79
kathakali 28
kilts 25
kings and queens 19, 29
koalas 50
Komodo dragons 52
krill 55

L

La Rinconada 20
lakes 78, 81
land reclamation 62
landslides 69
languages 22
laws 19
leap years 6
leaves 28, 50, 61, 63, 64, 66,
   68, 69
Lent 24, 25
life, beginning of 16
life on other planets 10, 16
light 8, 39, 41, 45
lightbulbs 43
light rays 45
lightning 16, 43
limestone 74
liquids 36, 39
liver 89
living stones 66
lizards 50, 52
llamas 32
locomotives 34

London 34
lunar eclipses 9
lunar months 6
lungs 88, 89
lungwort 63

M

Magellan, Ferdinand 33
magma 74
magnetism 13
malaria 63
mammals 48, 53, 69, 73
mandrills 52
mantle, Earth's 75
Maoris 26, 33
maple syrup 64
marble 74
marine mammals 53
Mars 7, 10
marshes 67
marsupials 48
mass 5, 37, 42
mastabas 30
matter 12, 13, 36
Matterhorn 81
Maya 32
meadowsweet 63
medicinal plants 62, 63, 70
megacities 20
melanin 84
Mercury 6, 7, 8, 10
metals 5, 38, 43
metamorphic rocks 74
mice 48
Middle Ages 25, 32
Milky Way 5, 11, 13, 16
minerals 74, 79
mistletoe 60
mixtures 38
Mojave Desert 66
molecular clouds 15, 16
molecules 37, 38, 39, 44, 45, 46
momentum 42
Mongols 32
monkeys 50, 52
months 6
Moon 6, 7, 8, 9, 42
moonlight 9

moral codes 23
Morris dancing 25
Mount Everest 68
Mount Fuji 81
mountains 66, 68–69, 75, 79, 81
Muhammad, Prophet 32
mummies 30
muscles 83, 86, 87, 88
Muslims 24, 32

N

nails 84
narwhals 56
national anthems 19
national parks 81
nations 17
Native Americans 25, 33
natural wonders 80–81
Navajo people 27
Neanderthals 73
nebulae 15
Needles 81
Neptune 6, 7, 10
nerves 85, 87
Netherlands 26
neutrons 37
new moons 9
New Zealand 26, 33
newt 56
Nile River 29
nitrogen 12, 39, 40, 43
Nobel Prizes 40
noble gases 37
nomads 32
noodles 27
North America 33, 50, 67
nuclear fusion 15, 44
nuclei 37

O

oases 66
okapis 48
Olympic Games 31
optics 45
organic chemistry 16, 38
ospreys 58
owls 57, 58

oxbow lakes 78
oxygen 10, 12, 35, 39, 40, 60,
  62, 70, 72, 88

P

paddies 67
pain relief 63
Pakistan 24
pampas 67
Panama hats 28
Papua New Guinea 27
parasitic plants 60, 61
Paris 28
parliaments 19, 20
parrots 57
Parsis 24
Parthenon 21
particle accelerators 13
particles 8, 36, 37, 45, 85
pelicans 58
penguins 58
peregrine falcons 58
periodic table 37
periwinkle 63
pharaohs 29, 30
photons 45
photosynthesis 59, 60
Pilgrims 33
pitch 46
planets 5, 6–7, 8, 10
plant oils 64
plants 59–64, 66, 67, 69, 70, 72
plasma 89
plates, Earth's 75, 76
Pleiades 14
polar bears 51, 52
pollination 69
pollution 67, 82
Polo, Marco 27
popping (ears) 87
pores 84
porpoises 46, 56
pow-wows 25
power 42
prairies 67
presidents 19
pressure 38, 39, 46
prickly pears 66

primates 48
proteins 16
protons 37, 40, 43
provinces 18
Proxima Centauri 15
puffins 58
pulsars 14
pyramids 30
pythons 52

Q

Qatar 20
quartz 74
quinine 63

R

radioactivity 40
radium 40
rafflesia 61
railroads 34
rain forests 48, 70, 82
rain shadows 66
rainbows 45
rainfall 70, 82
Ramadan 24
rattlesnakes 49
red dwarfs 14
red giants 14
religions 23–24, 32, 33
reptiles 48
republics 19
resistance 43
resistance 43
resonance 46
rhinos 47, 48
rice 67
rivers 78, 82
Rocket (locomotive) 34
rocks 5, 74, 75, 77, 78, 79
rodents 48, 49, 52
Roman Catholic Church 21
Roman Empire 32
Romans 25, 27, 31
roots 61, 62, 69
royal families 20
Russian Federation 20
Rutherford, Ernest 40

S

Sahara Desert 66
sailfish 54
St. Patrick's Day 26
St. Petersburg 28
sand pictures 27
sandstone 74
sap 60
satellites 22, 76
Saturn 7, 10
Saturnalia 25
Scotland 25, 27
sea levels 82
sea lions 53, 54, 55
seals 53, 55
seawater 39
seaweed 25
sedimentary rocks 74
seeds 61
Senegal 28
senses 85
sewage 34, 62, 82
sharks 54, 55
Shinto 24
shoots 61
sign language 22
Sikhs 24
silicon 12
silicon chips 43
sing-sings 27
skeleton 86
skin 84
skinks 50
skull 86
smell receptors 85
smogs 82
snakes 49, 50, 51, 52
soil fertility 62, 67, 70
Solar Cycle 8
solar eclipses 8
solar flares 8
solar power 41
solar system 5–10
solar wind 8
solids 36, 39
sound 46, 87
sound waves 46

South Africa 20
South America 32, 50, 70
Spain 26, 32
speed 42
spiders 26
spiral galaxies 13
spits 79
spyhopping 56
squirrels 48
stacks 79, 81
stalagmites 80
standard candles 15
stars 5, 7, 8, 11, 12, 14–15
states 17, 18
steam power 34
steel drums 27
Stephenson, George 34
steppes 67
stromatolites 72
substances 35, 36, 37, 38
succulents 66
sugars 60
summer 8
Sun 5, 6, 7, 8, 9, 14, 15, 41, 44,
    45, 60, 68, 84
sunsets 8
sunspots 8
superclusters 13
superconductors 43
supergiants 15
supernovae 15
sushi 25
swamps 67
sweating 84, 88

T

tadpoles 56
talking 88
Tao 24
Tasmanian devils 48
taste 85
tea 64
teeth 48, 49, 55
temperate regions 67
temperatures 10, 12, 44, 68
temples 21, 24, 31
tents 33

thermometers 44
tigers 49, 52
toads 54
Tokyo 20
touch 85
trace fossils 74
transits 8
transpiration 62
tree line 68
trees 64, 66, 68, 69, 70, 82
tributary rivers 78
tropicbirds 58
Turkey 26
turning force 42
turtles 55
tusking 56
tusks 47, 51, 56

U

ungulates 48
uniform motion 42
uniforms 28
United States 19, 22, 25, 27,
    80, 81
Universe 12–13, 16
Uranus 7, 10
urine 88, 89

V

Vatican City 21
veld 67
velocity 42
Venus 7, 8, 10
Venus flytraps 60
vibrations 46, 87, 88
Victoria Falls 80
Vikings 20
vincristine 63
vision 45, 85, 87
vocal cords 88
volcanoes 76
volts 43
volume (mass) 36
volume (sound) 46

W

walruses 53, 55

Walton, Ernest 40

water 10, 35, 39, 43, 61, 62, 79

water vapor 39, 62, 70

waterfalls 78, 80

Watson, James 40

wavelengths 45

waves 79

waxing and waning 9

weathering 77, 79, 80

weight 42

wetlands 67

whales 46, 54, 55, 56

whistling 22

white dwarfs 14

wildcats 50

Wilkins, Maurice 40

willows 63

winds 10

wolves 50, 51

wombats 48

Y

years 6

yeast 39

yucca plants 66

Z

Zeus 31

Zoroastrianism 24

ACKNOWLEDGMENTS

t = top, b = bottom, l = left, r = right, m = middle

Cover images courtesy of Shutterstock.com
and istock.com.

Getty Images
20-21 Johnny Haglund/Getty Images, 27b Oliver Strewe/Getty
Images, 36b Panoramic Images/Getty Images, 40tr Hulton
Archive/Getty Images, 40ml Hulton Archive/Getty Images,
65 J.A. Kraulis/Getty Images, 66m National Geographic/Getty
Images, 107 Library of Congress - Oren Jack Turner/Getty
Images.

Shutterstock.com
1bl Kletr/Shutterstock.com, 25b PKOM/Shutterstock.com,
26bl Patricia Hofmeester/Shutterstock.com.

istock.com
56l Dolphin/Rpsycho/istock.com.